"The doctrine of union with Christ declares to us Christians that God has so removed every barrier that we are forever safe within the total salvation that Christ has accomplished. Pastor Brad Wetherell invites us into this strong assurance. May your heart be thrilled by all that is now yours in Christ!"

Ray Ortlund, President, Renewal Ministries

"With so many different approaches to spiritual formation presented to Christians today, it's easy to lose sight of a basic but crucial question: What is the true source of our growth in the Christian life? In *Saved to Sin No More*, Brad Wetherell addresses this question by identifying, defining, and exploring the biblical reality that only through union with Christ can we become more like Christ. With the heart of a pastor and the precision of a theologian, Wetherell demonstrates how union with Christ undergirds our fight against sin and our pursuit of real righteousness. Drawing richly from both Scripture and the wisdom of saints who have gone before, *Saved to Sin No More* will be an encouragement to every Christian."

Matthew C. Bingham, Vice President of Academic Affairs and Associate Professor of Church History, Phoenix Seminary; author, *A Heart Aflame for God*

"Brad Wetherell has written a clear and compelling introduction to what may be the least understood and most vital reality of the Christian life. Union with Christ makes progress in our battle against sin possible, and any teaching that misses this dynamic will only be another version of self-help. This book will deepen your appreciation of all that is yours in Christ. It will give you hope, and it will spur you on in your pursuit of a holy life."

Colin S. Smith, President, Open the Bible; Pastor Emeritus, The Orchard, Arlington Heights, Illinois

"The doctrine of our union with Christ is, as Brad Wetherell tells us, both a 'joy-producing' and 'holiness-producing' doctrine. Resting firmly on careful biblical work, especially on the profound and beautiful chapters of Romans 5 and 6, Wetherell has provided not just a much-needed understanding of the implications of our union with Christ, but, even more, he has provided much-needed encouragement for our daily lives as Christ followers. There is no Christian who is not in need of the help this book supplies."

Mike Bullmore, Founding Pastor, CrossWay Community Church, Bristol, Wisconsin

"Brad Wetherell has written an extraordinary book that will help ordinary Christians understand and embrace the significance of their union with Christ."

Robert L. Plummer, Collin and Evelyn Aikman Professor of Biblical Studies, The Southern Baptist Theological Seminary

Saved to Sin No More

Saved to Sin No More

How Union with Christ Empowers a Life of Holiness

Brad Wetherell

Foreword by David Mathis

CROSSWAY®
WHEATON, ILLINOIS

Saved to Sin No More: How Union with Christ Empowers a Life of Holiness

Published by Crossway
1300 Crescent Street
Wheaton, Illinois 60187

This book draws from Brad Wetherell, "Teaching the Doctrine of Union with Christ at the Orchard in Arlington Heights, Illinois" (DMin project, Southern Baptist Theological Seminary, 2022), Boyce Digital Repository (103926728). Used by permission.

Cover design: David Fassett

Cover images: Getty Images

First printing 2026

Printed in the United States of America

All emphases in Scripture quotations have been added by the author.

Trade paperback ISBN: 979-8-8749-0046-5
ePub ISBN: 979-8-8749-0048-9
PDF ISBN: 979-8-8749-0047-2

Library of Congress Cataloging-in-Publication Data

Names: Wetherell, Brad, 1987– author.
Title: Saved to sin no more : how union with Christ empowers a life of holiness / Brad Wetherell ; foreword by David Mathis.
Description: Wheaton, Illinois : Crossway, 2026 | Includes bibliographical references and index.
Identifiers: LCCN 2025005603 (print) | LCCN 2025005604 (ebook) | ISBN 9798874900465 (trade paperback) | ISBN 9798874900472 (pdf) | ISBN 9798874900489 (epub)
Subjects: LCSH: Bible. Romans—Criticism, interpretation, etc. | Sin—Biblical teaching. | Mystical union—Biblical teaching. | Sin—Christianity.
Classification: LCC BS2665.52 .W444 2026 (print) | LCC BS2665.52 (ebook)
LC record available at https://lccn.loc.gov/2025005603
LC ebook record available at https://lccn.loc.gov/2025005604

Crossway is a publishing ministry of Good News Publishers.

BP 35 34 33 32 31 30 29 28 27 26
15 14 13 12 11 10 9 8 7 6 5 4 3 2 1

To Kristen,
with whom I am joyfully united in this life.

Dear dying Lamb, Thy precious blood
Shall never lose its power,
Till all the ransomed church of God
Be saved, to sin no more.

WILLIAM COWPER
"There Is a Fountain Filled with Blood"

Contents

Foreword

I FOUND A NEW FRIEND in the pages of this book. I hope you will too.

Brad and I have swapped emails, but we're yet to meet face to face. I look forward to that. But being in the same room isn't a prerequisite for friendship. A book such as this can tell you enough about a person—whether you have the most important things in common. Brad and I do.

For one, we share many of the same heroes of the faith—whether beloved dead dads such as Calvin, Newton, Tolkien, and Lewis, or still-living legends such as Carson, Schreiner, and Sinclair. Not only is Brad's writing concrete, teeming with illustrations, stories, and real life, but Brad quotes these shared heroes freely. He isn't so vain as to pretend to stand on his own two feet alone. Of course, the biblical text is the main rock, and beyond that, Brad readily hands the mic over to worthy men of previous generations and happily stands on their shoulders. And I love that one of my more recent personal favorites, J. C. Ryle, makes a prominent cameo at the end of the book.

Speaking of the end, the main thing Brad and I share is no *thing* at all but rather is our capital-*H* Hero. This is really why I found a new friend in Brad. The "thing" of union with Christ clearly serves the enjoyment of the person to whom this union connects us. Union, for Brad, is relational.

I would not be giving away the end but rather would be helping you read your way there most fruitfully if I told you as clear as day where this whole study is headed. Brad placards the conclusion with exactly the right banner for a book on union with Christ: Philippians 3:8–11. Do you, like the apostle Paul, long to *know* Jesus? Do you want to enjoy, and keep enjoying, the surpassing worth of *knowing* Jesus?

Union with Christ—being "found in him" (Phil. 3:9)—serves the daily communion of knowing and enjoying Christ (Phil. 3:8, 10). As Brad says, "The greatest gift of union with Christ is Christ himself." God made us to magnify his Son by enjoying him forever, and that begins right now. Jesus has given us his word (in Scripture), his ear (in prayer), his people (in the covenant community of the local church), and his Spirit (dwelling in us), who unites us to Christ and enables life-giving, soul-satisfying communion with him. The person of Christ comes first (and last), then comes the concept of union with him, serving a living relationship with him. We don't subordinate the person to the union. Union supports our love of and delight in the person.

I know that the *doctrine of union with Christ* sounds thrilling to some ears and *meh* to others. If *union with Christ* seems boring to you, it may be because your previous exposure was too transactional and not sufficiently relational. Perhaps the emphasis was on the union, on the exchange, or on the goods, but not on the person.

The reason that some of us get so excited about union with Christ is that this doctrine brings all of Christ's benefits back to Christ himself. He's a person, not a portfolio. He's our brother, not a bank. Salvation is no mere transaction, but a deliverance *from* sin and death and a rescue *to* real life forever with the all-satisfying person for whom our souls were made.

So Brad and I also share a love for holiness. You cannot love such a Christ and not come to delight in being more like him through being empowered by him. As Brad says, union with Christ is not only exhilarating and joy-producing but holiness-producing. Come see why true holiness and real happiness aren't two diverging roads but are one and the same path—in union with Christ.

David Mathis
Senior teacher and executive
editor, Desiring God
Author, *Habits of Grace: Enjoying Jesus*
Through the Spiritual Disciplines
Saint Paul, Minnesota

Acknowledgments

I FEEL A PROFOUND SENSE of gratitude as I wrap up this project. First, I'm thankful for my church. In more ways than I could possibly mention, serving in pastoral ministry at the Orchard is a tremendous privilege and joy.

Several people at the Orchard have played a unique part in helping this book come to its final form. For as long as I've known him, Colin Smith has helped me fix my eyes on Christ and the wonders of union with him. As this project developed over the years, Colin offered significant insight and encouragement. Without his support, this book would never have come about. Jason and Heather English, Josh Parsons, and Michael Porter read each chapter, offering thoughtful comments that greatly improved this work.

Before *Saved to Sin No More* was a book idea, it was a doctor of ministry project.[1] I continue to thank God for the wise counsel and guidance that Rob Plummer provided as my supervisor. Dr. Plummer was also the first to suggest that I consider publishing the material.

That publishing journey began with Champ Thornton's kindness to hear my idea, help me form it into a proposal, and bring it to the team at Crossway. Partnering with Crossway has been wonderful. I'm thankful for the perceptive editorial eye of Samuel James and Becca Davis. There is no question that this book is better because of their good work.

Of course, I want to express my deep love and gratitude for my family. My parents and parents-in-law offer support in so many ways, but I am especially thankful for their prayers. My kids, Joanna, John, and Lydia, bring such delight and light to my life, and I pray each day that they might enjoy every spiritual blessing found in Christ. Kristen is my best editor, my best friend, and the love of my life. I cannot thank her enough for all her help throughout this project.

1 Brad Wetherell, "Teaching the Doctrine of Union with Christ at the Orchard in Arlington Heights, Illinois" (DMin project, Southern Baptist Theological Seminary, 2022), Boyce Digital Repository (103926728).

Finally, above all, I am eternally grateful to Jesus Christ, who is my life. "Indeed, I count everything as loss because of the surpassing worth of knowing Christ Jesus my Lord" (Phil. 3:8).

Introduction

Blessed be the God and Father of our Lord Jesus Christ, who has blessed us in Christ with every spiritual blessing.

EPHESIANS 1:3

THIS IS A BOOK about doctrine.

Doctrine. What comes into your mind when you hear that word? Perhaps it excites you. You love diving deep into biblical studies, mining the Scriptures for treasures of truth. You enjoy listening to trusted voices from the past, gleaning insights from our brothers and sisters throughout church history. Your bookshelves are full of resources marked up with notes and highlights.

My guess is, however, that some of you have a different reaction to the word *doctrine*. It's not that you think doctrine is unimportant. It's just, well, something you'd rather let other people worry about. You're glad that pastors and professors take time to study theology, but you're content to leave that to the professionals. If you're honest, the thought of reading about doctrine sounds a bit boring.

So why read this book? After all, this is a book about doctrine—the doctrine of union with Christ.

I think D. Martyn Lloyd-Jones says it best. He writes that the doctrine of union with Christ is "one of the most glorious aspects of the Christian truth, one of the most profound, one of the most stimulating, one of the most comforting—indeed I rather like to use the word exhilarating."[1] Doctrine? Exhilarating? Yes. Let me show you why.

The Blessing We Enjoy

When I was in junior high, our school band won the most prestigious competition in the state of Illinois: the SuperState Concert Band Festival. Technically, this makes me an award-winning tenor saxophone player. But you don't want to hear me play. The truth is, I barely squeaked by (pun intended) in auditions, rehearsals, and concerts. I wasn't any good, but I was in a band with people who were. I only enjoyed

1 D. Martyn Lloyd-Jones, *Romans 6: The New Man* (Banner of Truth, 1972), 30.

the blessing of that SuperState victory because I was united with the band.

As Christians we enjoy tremendous blessing. We have peace with God because he has forgiven our sins. We have unshakable hope because he has a home for us in heaven. We have power to endure the trials of life because his Spirit dwells within us. But this occurs only if we are united with Christ.

John Calvin says,

> We must understand that as long as Christ remains outside of us, and we are separated from him, all that he has suffered and done for the salvation of the human race remains useless and of no value to us.[2]

According to Calvin, if we are not united with Christ, we receive no benefit from Christ, and everything he did makes no difference for us.

That's a bold statement. But is it a biblical statement?

If you open your favorite Bible app and type "union with Christ" into the search bar, do you know how many results will appear? Zero. The phrase *union with Christ* does not

2 John Calvin, *Institutes of the Christian Religion*, ed. John T. McNeill, trans. Ford Lewis Battles, Library of Christian Classics 20–21 (Westminster John Knox, 2011), 1:537.

appear a single time in any English translation that I am aware of. Romans 6:5 comes very close when it says that we have been "united with him," but that's it.

So how can a phrase that never appears in the Bible be so vitally important? Plenty of significant theological terms never appear in the biblical text. For example, you won't find the word *Trinity* in the Bible, but that doesn't mean we toss that doctrine aside. The word *Trinity* is a theological term that expresses a key biblical reality.

Similarly, the phrase *union with Christ* may not appear in the Scriptures, but the doctrine sure does. In fact, it appears so frequently and so pervasively that we often read right past it without noticing it. It shows up repeatedly in the two words *in Christ*. That phrase, or some variation of it—such as *in him* or *with him*—appears hundreds of times in the New Testament, and it often refers to the doctrine of union with Christ.

A few years ago, my wife and I were shopping for a new car, and we began to set our sights on a Volkswagen SUV. Before we started shopping, I didn't even know that Volkswagen made an SUV. But once we started thinking about buying one, I saw them everywhere.

And once you start looking for the words *in Christ* in the New Testament, you'll see them everywhere. For example, look at this passage from the beginning of Ephesians:

> Blessed be the God and Father of our Lord Jesus Christ, who has blessed us *in Christ* with every spiritual blessing in the heavenly places. . . . *In him* we have redemption through his blood, the forgiveness of our trespasses, according to the riches of his grace . . .
>
> *In him* we have obtained an inheritance. . . . *In him* you . . . were sealed with the promised Holy Spirit. (Eph. 1:3, 7, 11, 13)

Do you see the significance? Every spiritual blessing comes to us *in Christ.* Our redemption, our forgiveness, and all the grace we enjoy is ours *in him.* Our eternal inheritance is secure *in him.* We are sealed with the Holy Spirit *in him.* Even if we had only these verses from Ephesians, we would have reason to recognize the importance of union with Christ.

As we meditate on this doctrine, our hearts will well up with gratitude for the blessing God has shown us in Christ. It is an exhilarating, joy-producing doctrine. It is also a holiness-producing doctrine.

The Power We Need

All of us are wrestling with sin. In case you weren't aware, the church is full of stumbling, struggling saints. Not one of us is perfect. We know that God calls us to pursue holiness, but we also know that this isn't easy. Sin trips us up, causes us to fall, and ensnares us.

In this battle, we become prone to two opposite mistakes. The first mistake is the slide toward legalism. This happens when we see our sin, know it's a problem, and want to do something about it. But we think that the sole solution is found in exerting more effort, mustering up more resolve, and practicing more discipline. So with white knuckles and gritted teeth, we strive for a self-righteousness that we will never attain. This leads to frustration, pride, and all kinds of problems.

The second mistake is the drift into apathy. This happens when we see our sin, know it's a problem, and trust that God has done something about it. But we begin to think that the gospel basically amounts to the truth that Jesus pardons sinners, so we don't exert much effort in fighting sin. We resign ourselves to the way things are as we declare our dependence on God's grace. We become lazy about resisting temptation, and we grow far too content with certain sinful patterns.

Do you recognize yourself in either scenario? If you do, you're not alone. These mistakes leave many Christians either anxiously trying to earn God's favor or complacent in their sinful habits. So what will help? A better understanding of union with Christ.

As we grow in our grasp of this doctrine, we will discover that we are acceptable in God's sight only because of our relationship to God's Son. Apart from him, we are hopelessly lost. But in union with him, we enter a whole new position. In Christ, we are justified. We are clothed with his righteousness, and nothing can change this status.

Therefore, we pursue holiness not to earn God's favor but because he has already lavished his favor on us. We belong to him (Rom. 14:8). We are saved by his grace (Eph. 2:8). And we live without any fear of condemnation (Rom. 8:1). Every Christian prone to legalism needs to hear this liberating news—it's all part of being united with Christ.

But if we are justified in Christ by no effort of our own, why can't we go on sinning, knowing that grace will abound (Rom. 6:1)? The answer is that in Christ, God not only pardons us; he also transforms us.

In Christ, we are not the people we used to be. We are not stuck in bondage to sin; rather, we are set free for a whole new life with him (Rom. 6:22). Having been saved by his grace, we are now set apart for his glory (1 Pet. 2:9). Having been justified, we are now being sanctified (1 Thess. 5:23). Every Christian prone to apathy needs to hear this crucial news—it's all part of being united with Christ.

Union with Christ means we are saved. It also means we are saved to sin no more.

This reality should fill us with comfort. We won't attain perfection in this life, but there is real hope for real change. You are not hopelessly stuck in sin; you are in Christ. And union with Christ empowers a life of holiness. It also guarantees the life to come.

The Security We Desire

You cannot be a Christian without faith. But you can be a Christian without assurance of salvation. There are seasons of the Christian life when doubt or despair impede our sense of assurance like clouds covering the sun. Many times, our ongoing struggle with sin is a source of this discouragement. And yet just as the sun hidden behind the clouds is still shining, a true Christian whose assurance is hidden is still saved.

How do you get that sense of security and assurance if you do not feel it? There are many biblical answers to this question, but none is more foundational than union with Christ. As Lloyd-Jones writes, "There is nothing, perhaps, in the whole range and realm of doctrine which, if properly grasped and understood, gives greater assurance, greater comfort, and greater hope than this doctrine of our union with Christ."[3]

Why is that true? It's true because when God brings you into union with Christ, he will not let you out.

In Christ, we are justified. In Christ, we are being sanctified. And in Christ, we will be glorified (Rom. 8:30). The more you understand union with Christ, the more you will rest assured that "neither death nor life, nor angels nor rulers, nor things present nor things to come, nor powers, nor height nor depth, nor anything else in all creation, will be able to separate us from the love of God *in Christ Jesus our Lord*" (Rom. 8:38–39).

Union with Christ is the source of every spiritual blessing, the power for the pursuit of holiness, and the bedrock of assurance. As we explore what it means to be in Christ throughout this book, I hope you will come to see the grace of God more clearly, fight sin more confidently, and rest in your salvation more completely.

A Preview of What's to Come

At this point you might be thinking, "That sounds great, but what exactly *is* union with Christ?"

3 Lloyd-Jones, *Romans 6*, 30.

As I've studied this doctrine, I've found that everyone seems to agree on two things. First, union with Christ is very important. Second, union with Christ is very difficult to define. I have no desire to oversimplify the doctrine, but I do want to give you a definition you can remember.

So here's the definition that we explore in this book: *Union with Christ refers to the believer's position in Christ established at conversion, experienced in all of life, and enjoyed forever.*

I've developed this definition from one primary passage of Scripture: Romans 5:12–6:23. These are some of the most important verses in the Bible that teach the doctrine of union with Christ (though they are certainly not the only ones). So with support from other scriptures, Romans 5:12–6:23 serves as the main text for the chapters that follow.

Here's a preview of what's to come.

Chapter 1 examines what Romans 6:1–4 teaches us about the moment we come into union with Christ. At conversion, our lives are plunged into Christ. We become so identified with Christ that we can now say we died and rose with Christ. His story becomes our story. Therefore, no Christian has a dull testimony. And the more we understand the transformation God has brought about in our lives, the more awestruck gratitude we will feel.

Chapter 2 returns to Romans 5:12–21 and outlines some of the rich theological truths behind every Christian conversion. We were once hopeless and helpless—we were condemned before God, ruled by sin, and destined for everlasting death. But salvation brings us into a whole new position. Now in Christ, we are justified before God, ruled by grace, and destined for everlasting life.

Chapters 3–5 discuss how union with Christ affects our experience in all of life. Romans 6:5–19 calls us to consider ourselves dead to sin and alive to God in Christ Jesus. Because we have been crucified with Christ, our old lives in bondage to sin are over. Because we have been raised with Christ, our new lives in service to God have begun. In Christ, we are new creations with new ability to resist sin and pursue holiness. If you're worn down and weary in the battle against sin, I pray that these chapters are particularly encouraging to you.

Chapter 6 helps us see that our union with Christ is something that we will enjoy forever. Romans 6:20–23 serves as a wonderful source of assurance and a glorious crescendo of Paul's explanation of union with Christ. "Eternal life," he says, is "in Christ Jesus our Lord" (6:23). Our union with Christ is never going to end. We are safe and secure in him. And the permanence of this union fuels our everlasting hope and joy.

Finally, chapter 7 describes the crucial role of the church in our sanctification. Union with Christ is a deeply personal reality, but it is also the shared reality of all God's people. As brothers and sisters in Christ, we have the responsibility to bear one another's burdens and build one another up. We are called to grow together.

So yes, this is a book about doctrine—an exhilarating doctrine. Understanding your union with Christ will increase your joy, empower your pursuit of holiness, and strengthen your assurance. My prayer is that as you read these pages, you will find your heart stirred by all that is yours in Christ.

1

Saved to Die

What shall we say then? Are we to continue in sin that grace may abound? By no means! How can we who died to sin still live in it? Do you not know that all of us who have been baptized into Christ Jesus were baptized into his death? We were buried therefore with him by baptism into death, in order that, just as Christ was raised from the dead by the glory of the Father, we too might walk in newness of life.

ROMANS 6:1–4

"I WANT TO TELL YOU how I stopped being [a dragon]."[1] So begins the testimony of a boy named Eustace Clarence Scrubb. Eustace had been a miserable boy with a miserly spirit. Then,

1 C. S. Lewis, *The Voyage of the Dawn Treader* (HarperCollins, 2008), chap. 7, Kindle.

one night, "sleeping on a dragon's hoard with greedy, dragonish thoughts in his heart, he had become a dragon himself."[2] And a dragon he remained—until he met a lion.

The lion came to Eustace, tore off his scales, washed him in a well of living water, and turned him into a boy again. Eustace was never the same. From that day forward, he "began to be a different boy. He had relapses. There were still many days when he could be very tiresome. But . . . the cure had begun."[3]

What's Your Story?

Union with Christ refers to the believer's position in Christ *established at conversion.* Every Christian has a conversion story—a testimony. If I asked you to share yours, how would you begin?

Maybe, like Eustace, you'd start by saying, "I want to tell you how I stopped being a dragon." Only, instead of "dragon," you'd insert some other label that clearly communicated the corruption of your former life. You'd readily admit that you were a slave to some deep darkness. And you'd joyfully attest to the way that Jesus came and set you free. Your story is dramatic.

2 Lewis, *Dawn Treader,* chap. 6.

3 Lewis, *Dawn Treader,* chap. 7.

But maybe, like many believers I know, you'd start by saying, "I grew up in a Christian home." You'd go on to describe how you came to faith at a young age. You'd share some struggles you had as a teenager or a young adult. But then you'd talk about a time when you recommitted your life to Jesus and describe how you've walked with him ever since. Your story is a lot like mine.

And there is a temptation for anyone with a story like the second one. If we're not careful, we can begin to think that there wasn't much saving Jesus really needed to do for us. After all, though we wouldn't put it this bluntly, we know other people who have sinned way more and way worse than we ever have. So we might find ourselves looking at others with pride.

Or, strange as it may sound, we might find ourselves looking at others with envy. Their stories are so exciting. Their experience of God's grace is so obviously transformative. And in comparison, our stories sound dull.

Here's what I want you to take away from this chapter: If you listen to other believers' testimonies with either pride or envy, it can only mean that you have not yet grasped the extent of Jesus's saving work on your behalf.

The truth is, you and I do not need any less saving than anyone else, so there is no room for pride. You and I have also not received any less saving than anyone else, so there is no reason for envy.

"Dull testimony" is an oxymoron. Every salvation story is dramatic. Every one is a story of death and resurrection.

Your Story Is Jesus's Story

"Do you not know that all of us who have been baptized into Christ Jesus were baptized into his death?" (Rom. 6:3).

Do you not know? This is something Paul expects every believer in Rome to understand. This is not doctoral-level theology for elite scholars to muse on in their ivory towers. This is truth to encourage every believer: We have been baptized into Christ Jesus.

What does that mean?

Consider one pattern of conversion to Christianity. Someone hears the gospel, responds in repentance and faith, and then publicly professes that faith through baptism. When Paul talks about baptism in Romans 6, he's talking about all this. He's using baptism as a single word to describe the whole conversion experience. And he says that when we become Christians, we are not simply baptized into water, we are baptized into Christ.

When we come to faith in Christ, our lives are plunged into Christ. And in this union with Christ, something remarkable happens: We become so identified with Christ that we can now say we died and rose with him. His story becomes our story.

We Died with Christ

We know Jesus's story. He was crucified, died, and was buried. But did you know that when you came to believe in him, you were buried with him? Paul says, "We were buried therefore with him by baptism into death" (Rom. 6:4).

I was baptized in high school, and it was largely uneventful. I stepped into a warm pool on the stage in our sanctuary. I answered a few brief questions. I went under the water and came back out again. No one called the paramedics. There was no need for CPR. There certainly wasn't a funeral a few days later.

So what is Paul talking about when he connects baptism with burial? What does he mean when he says we died with Christ when we came to faith in Christ? I've found it helpful to think about this both from God's perspective and from sin's perspective.

Dead in God's Eyes

When God looks at this world, what does he see? We don't have to guess:

The LORD looks down from heaven on the children
    of man,
  to see if there are any who understand,
  who seek after God.
They have all turned aside; together they have become
    corrupt;
  there is none who does good,
  not even one. (Ps. 14:2–3)

When God looks at this world, he sees all our rebellion, all our corruption, and all our sin. We might do a decent job of hiding our sin from others or ignoring our sin ourselves, but God sees all of it. And as the just Judge of the universe, one day he will punish all of it.

But if you are a Christian, when God looks at you, he sees you *in Christ*. At your conversion, your whole life was plunged into Christ. And since you are united with Christ, his story has become your story—including the story of his death.

This means that when God looks at you, even though he sees someone who deserves to die for sin, he now sees someone who has died already. From God's viewpoint, what happened to Jesus happened to you. His death has become your death. You are in Christ, and he paid the penalty so you never will.

Beginning on September 7, 1940, the German Luftwaffe bombed London fifty-six times in fifty-seven days. Day after day, night after night, when the air raid sirens blared, people went into shelters. And the bombs came crashing down. But if the shelters held up, everyone inside was spared.

If you are in Christ, the just judgment for your sin has already come crashing down. But it landed on Jesus's shoulders as he hung on the cross (1 Pet. 2:24). You have been spared. From God's perspective, you died with Christ. There is now no condemnation for you (Rom. 8:1).

Dead in Sin's Eyes

When sin looks at this world, what does it see? That may sound strange. Does sin really *see* anything? Throughout the Bible, we see that sin does not merely consist in our personal failures. Sin is also a powerful force. It's a force that Scripture sometimes personifies.

For example, the Bible says that sin crouched at the doorway of Cain's life, watching carefully for an opportunity to rule over him (Gen. 4:7). Sin gained mastery over humanity, enslaving us all (John 8:34). And sin is the power that has reigned throughout history, causing chaos and destruction (Rom. 5:21).

You can think of sin as a wicked tyrant seated on a terrible throne, looking out on this fallen world. Sin sees a captive humanity suffering under his dark reign in a corrupted creation. But that's not all. Sin also sees some who have escaped. They have left his dominion in the only way possible: They have died.

When we die, we leave one realm and enter another. Death does not send us into oblivion, ending our existence. Death is a departure that brings us to a new destination. And when we were united with Christ, we left sin's dominion. We "died to sin" (Rom. 6:2).

At funerals, you often hear people say, "We lost him," or, "She passed away." Similarly, if you are in Christ, sin could say the same things about you. When you were converted, sin lost you. When you were united with Christ, you passed away from the realm of sin's power.

From sin's perspective, you died with Christ. Sin no longer rules over you.

Two Common Objections

At this point, I want to address two common objections people raise when they hear this sort of teaching. The first typically comes from skeptical unbelievers, and it goes something like this: If there is no condemnation for those who are in Christ Jesus, if God's grace is really that abundant, then what will keep Christians from sinning?

I remember taking a taxi home from O'Hare International Airport several years ago and striking up a conversation with the driver. He was a nice man and a committed Muslim. When he found out I was a pastor, he was eager to talk about our different faiths, and he shared one of his major objections to Christianity: "You believe God will forgive you no matter what you do," he said, "and therefore, you'll live however you want." He was convinced that abundant grace must lead to abundant sin.

But Paul says the exact opposite. Yes, God's grace is abundant. In fact, where sin increases, grace abounds all the more (Rom. 5:20). Every time we sin, God has an opportunity to reveal the glory of his grace. But does that mean we should "continue in sin that grace may abound?" Paul's answer is emphatic: "By no means!" (6:1–2).

Why not? When we were converted, we were united with Christ. We died with Christ. And when we died with Christ, we died to sin (6:2). As my taxi driver recognized, this means that there is no condemnation for us. But this also means that sin has lost its mastery over us. We have been set free from sin's dark power, and there's no going back. We cannot live as if nothing has changed. We cannot go on willfully, unrepentantly living in sin.

But that brings me to the second objection, which is most often raised by discouraged believers. It goes something like this: If I am dead to sin, why do I still struggle with sin? If my captivity to sin's tyranny is over, why do I still give in to sin's demands? I know myself. Sin tempts me every day, and I give in far more often than I want to admit. Does this mean that I'm not united with Christ after all?

Imagine two nations. One nation is ruled by an awful tyrant, and its citizens are miserable. The other nation is ruled by a benevolent king, and its citizens are blessed. We were once in the tyrant's realm. Sin ruled over us, and we had no hope of escape. But when God saved us, he pulled us out of sin's dominion and put us into the kingdom of his Son (Col. 1:13). He gave us new citizenship (Phil. 3:20), and there's no going back.

Yet as anyone who has ever moved to a new country can attest, it takes time to grow accustomed to a new culture. Old habits die hard. And even though we are citizens of Christ's kingdom, we struggle to put off our former ways of living. Sin still tempts us, trips us up, and causes us to fall. But here's the wonderful news: All that stumbling and sinning happens in our new country. And God does not deport us when we disobey. Our citizenship remains.

Therefore, when we are discouraged by our sin, we need to remember our position. We are in Christ. We are living under his reign. Sin will never rule over us again. Yes, it will continue to affect us and allure us. Yes, it will mar our experience in many ways. But our position remains. We are united with Christ. And in Christ, we are dead to sin because we died with him.

But that's not all. If Jesus's story is our story, then we have not only died. We have risen.

We Rose with Christ

When we are united with Christ, we become so identified with Christ that his story becomes our story. We can say that we died with Christ. And we can also say that we rose with Christ. For "just as Christ was raised from the dead by the glory of the Father, we too . . . walk in newness of life" (Rom. 6:4). When you tell your testimony, you are telling a story of resurrection. You are talking about a miracle.

The resurrection of Jesus is the epitome of a miracle. On that first Easter Sunday, a heart that had stopped for three days began to beat. Eyes that seemed closed for good opened once again. A dead man was raised to life. Christ's resurrection put the power of God on display as never before. And every Christian's conversion does the same thing.

God removed our hearts of stone and replaced them with hearts of flesh (Ezek. 36:26). God opened our blind eyes to show us the glory of his Son (2 Cor. 4:6). God caused us, who once walked in spiritual death, to rise to spiritual life (Eph. 2:5–6). In Christ, new life is not only our future hope—it is our present reality.

In 2 Corinthians, Paul declares that "if anyone is in Christ, he is a new creation. The old has passed away; behold, the new has come" (2 Cor. 5:17). Notice the tense of those verbs. Paul does not say, "If anyone is in Christ, he *will* be a new creation." He does not say, "The old *will* pass away and the new *will* come." He says it's already happened. In Christ, you are a new creation. Your old life has passed away. Your new life has begun.

Christians are not like eggs waiting to hatch. We are not hunkered down inside our shells, hanging in there until a future resurrection. We have emerged into a new life. And just like little birds, we've got a lot to learn. So we stumble around. We trip and fall. We don't take off flying right away. But we really do walk in newness of life.

The Cure Has Begun

Do you see why there is no such thing as a dull testimony? It doesn't matter if you were converted out of notorious, public wickedness or as a four-year-old in your Sunday School class. When God saved you, he united you with Christ. And Jesus's story has become your story.

Jesus died, and you died with him. Jesus rose, and you rose with him. And rising from the dead is as dramatic as it gets! Consider taking a moment right now to thank God for the magnitude of mercy he has poured out on you.

Every conversion is a miracle of his grace. And every conversion marks the beginning of a glorious transformation.

Christians are like Eustace. From the day the lion rescued him, he "began to be a different boy. He had relapses. There were still many days when he could be very tiresome. But . . . the cure had begun."[4] And from the day Jesus saves us, we become new creations. We are not yet perfect, but the cure has begun.

4 Lewis, *Dawn Treader*, chap. 7.

2

Saved to Rise

Therefore, as one trespass led to condemnation for all men, so one act of righteousness leads to justification and life for all men. For as by the one man's disobedience the many were made sinners, so by the one man's obedience the many will be made righteous.

ROMANS 5:18–19

CHARLES DICKENS'S classic novel *A Tale of Two Cities* tells the story of a French doctor, Alexandre Manette, who begins a new life in London after his release from prison in Paris. It's one man's story set against the backdrop of the much bigger story of the French Revolution.

Like Doctor Manette, we too have begun a new life after being released from prison. When God saved us, he rescued us from bondage to sin by uniting us with his beloved Son. We died with Christ and began a new life in Christ. And we all have our own conversion stories with unique details of how God saved us by his grace.

At the same time, as in *A Tale of Two Cities*, our individual stories are each set against the backdrop of a much bigger story. It's a story that goes back to the beginning of human history and will stretch out into eternity. It's an epic tale of ruin, rescue, and redemption. And we could call it *A Tale of Two Men.*

It's the story of Adam and Christ.

Two Types of People

Union with Christ refers to the believer's position in Christ established at conversion, experienced in all of life, and enjoyed forever. In this chapter, our focus is on the believer's position. What does it mean to be *in Christ*?

One of the key biblical passages that describes this position is Romans 5:12–21. It's a complex passage. But if you read it, which I encourage you to do right now, you can see one thing very clearly: Paul is drawing an important distinction between Adam and Christ.

Paul says that Adam was a "type" of person like Christ (5:14). The word for "type" means a certain kind, class, or pattern.[1] Adam is a kind of person like Christ. He's in the same class of person as Christ. He and Christ both fit a similar pattern.

So what type of person is Adam? What type of person is Christ? They are both representatives of the entire human race, and as such, their actions affect everyone whom they represent. Theologians sometimes refer to this as *headship*. Adam and Christ are the two heads of humanity. They are like two fathers leading two families. All of us belong to one or the other of these two families, and what our father has done affects us all.

Western culture is highly individualistic, so talking about representative figures affecting the whole human race may sound foreign to many of us. But we all know that the actions of a father have an effect on his entire family, for better or for worse. That's certainly true with Adam and Christ: "For as in Adam all die, so also in Christ shall all be made alive" (1 Cor. 15:22).

The story of Adam and Christ is the larger narrative within which all our personal stories take place. We were all born into Adam's family, enduring the ruin he brought on us. But

1 Frederick W. Danker, Walter Bauer, William F. Arndt, and F. Wilbur Gingrich, *Greek-English Lexicon of the New Testament and Other Early Christian Literature*, 3rd ed. (University of Chicago Press, 2000), under τύπος.

when we believed in Christ, we were born again into his family, enjoying the restoration he secured for us.

This is the believer's position. And the change could not be more significant. Coming into Christ's family shapes our standing before God, our relationship to sin, and our eternal future.

In Christ, We Have a New Verdict

In every TV courtroom drama, or during live coverage of an actual case, the climactic moment is the declaration of the verdict. A hush comes over the room as the judge shares his decision or the jury reveals their conclusion. Everyone waits to hear—is the defendant guilty or not?

If we were to stand in God's courtroom on our own, there's no question what verdict we would receive. We are guilty and we know it (Rom. 3:10, 23).

But here's what we may not know: Our guilty verdict was declared long before we were born. In the very beginning, "one trespass led to condemnation for all men" (5:18). Adam's single sin condemned us because Adam was our representative. He was the head of our household, and his failure affected his whole family.

Yes, we have committed many sins that confirm and contribute to the case against us. But before we ever rebelled against God ourselves, in Adam, we were condemned.

Now, you might be thinking, "That sounds like the worst possible news! I'm condemned for something that one man did thousands of years before I was born?" That's right. God gave Adam the unique position of representative. He failed, and we are all facing the consequences.

But the truth that God deals with us in light of what one man has done is equally the best possible news. There's another representative: Christ. And when we come into his family, we receive a whole new verdict.

Yes, it's true, "one trespass led to condemnation for all men." But it is also true that "one act of righteousness leads to justification and life for all men" (5:18). Adam's rebellious action, which occurred thousands of years before we were born, ruined us. But Jesus's righteous action, which also occurred thousands of years before we were born, redeemed us.

Jesus entered this sinful world, plunged himself beneath the waters of God's judgment, and rose again to bring us to safety (4:25).

Through his once-for-all sacrifice, Jesus paid the penalty our sins deserved and bore the wrath we should have faced (Heb. 9:25–28). Through his act of righteousness, Jesus made us righteous (Rom. 5:19; 2 Cor. 5:21). In Christ, we are no longer guilty in God's sight. *Justified* is our verdict now.

The implications of this truth could not be more wonderful. We have peace with God, access to his presence, and hope for the future (Rom. 5:1–2). We don't need to fear that God is against us. We can cast all our burdens on him in prayer. And though we live in this world full of sorrow, we never need to despair. For those whom God justifies, he glorifies, and nothing will separate us from the love he has for us in Christ (Rom. 8:30, 38–39).

When God saves us, he takes us out of Adam's family and transfers us into Christ's. And in this new position, we have a new verdict. But that's not all.

In Christ, We Have a New Ruler

So far I've been speaking about sin as something we do (or fail to do) that offends God and makes us guilty. That's the most common way we think about sin, and it's correct. But sin is not only the personal failures that make us guilty; sin is also a powerful force that makes us slaves.

Imagine a medieval castle with high walls, a drawbridge, and a moat. A hostile army approaches, but it can't get in. But then, tragically, someone inside the city lowers the bridge and opens the gate, allowing the enemy to rush inside.

This is what happened in the garden of Eden. Adam opened the door, and sin broke into this world. "Sin came into the world through one man" (Rom. 5:12).

And having entered the world, sin began to reign (5:21). We see the evidence of sin's reign all around us. Sin is the cause of every bit of disease, disaster, discord, decay, and death that plagues us. Creation itself groans in its bondage to corruption (8:20–22). And sin's throne is firmly fixed within the human heart.

We know this, even if it's hard to admit. Our hearts are deceptive and "desperately sick" (Jer. 17:9). Out of our hearts flows a whole host of evils (Matt. 15:19). No one needs to teach us pride, selfishness, anger, or lust. These things come naturally to us because sin rules over us.

Because Adam became a sinner, everyone in his family is born a sinner (Rom. 5:19). Sin reigns over everyone in Adam's family, defiling and dominating our very natures (Eph. 2:3). As Thomas Schreiner says, "There is something prior to individual sin, something that undergirds and explains it: because of Adam's sin, human beings enter the world spiritually dead."[2]

If you've ever sinned and thought, "Why in the world did I do that?" here's your answer: You and I sin because we are sinners.

2 Thomas R. Schreiner, *Romans*, 2nd ed., Baker Exegetical Commentary on the New Testament, ed. Joshua Jipp and Robert W. Yarbrough (Baker Academic, 2018), 289.

Many people disagree with this. Many people believe that humans are born in a state of neutrality, only to be corrupted by the evils of society. This is why so many people are passionately trying to fix society—they believe that if you save society, you will save humanity.

But that is a recipe for frustration because society is not the primary problem—we are. In 1905, G. K. Chesterton put it perfectly when he wrote to a newspaper to discuss what was wrong with the world in his day. He said, "The answer to the question, 'What is Wrong?' is, or should be, 'I am wrong.'"[3]

The Bible teaches that everyone who is born into Adam's family is born in a state of rebellion (Ps. 51:4–5). As we grow, we find countless ways to corrupt the world around us. We are what's wrong with the world because sin reigns over us.

But when we come into Christ's family, a new ruler takes the throne. None of us had the power to overthrow sin's tyrannical reign. We were slaves to sin, but Christ set us free (John 8:34–36; Rom. 6:20–22). Jesus stormed the castle of our hearts, kicked sin off the throne, and established his rule.

John Newton beautifully describes this in his hymn "The Castle of the Human Heart":

3 G. K. Chesterton, "What Is Wrong?," letter to the editor, *Daily News*, August 16, 1905.

The castle of the human heart
  Strong in its native sin,
Is guarded well, in every part,
  By him who dwells within. . . .

But Jesus, stronger far than he,
  In his appointed hour
Appears, to set his people free
  From the usurper's pow'r.

"This heart I bought with blood," he says,
  "And now it shall be mine";
His voice the strong one armed dismays,
  He knows he must resign.

In spite of unbelief and pride,
  And self, and Satan's art;
The gates of brass fly open wide,
  And Jesus wins the heart.[4]

When we are united with Christ, sin's reign over our hearts comes to an end, and we are set free. But we are not released

4 John Newton, "The Castle of the Human Heart," (1779), https://hymnary.org/.

into unfettered autonomy. Jesus wins the heart. He takes hold of our affections, and his grace begins to reign over our lives (Rom. 5:21). Newton captures this reality in the last verse of his hymn:

> The rebel soul that once withstood
> The Savior's kindest call;
> Rejoices now, by grace subdued,
> To serve him with her all.[5]

By the power of his grace, Jesus begins a process of repairing all the wreckage that sin caused. For "where sin increased, grace abounded all the more" (5:20). Grace truly is amazing. It is far more powerful than sin. Whatever sin has ruined, grace can do "all the more" to restore.

Grace restores our relationship with God. All our sinful actions, thoughts, and desires pile up to a mountain of guilt. We deserve punishment. But grace means we don't get what we deserve. We receive mercy. We receive pardon. Under the reign of his grace, God

> does not deal with us according to our sins,
> nor repay us according to our iniquities. . . .

5 Newton, "The Castle of the Human Heart."

as far as the east is from the west,
so far does he remove our transgressions from us.
(Ps. 103:10, 12)

Grace also transforms our sinful natures. We were born sinners, spiritually dead. But in his grace, God restores us. He causes us to be born again (1 Pet. 1:3). He gives us new life empowered by the Holy Spirit to flee from temptation and pursue godliness (Gal. 5:16).

And one day, grace will restore our sinful world. Right now, this world is full of chaos. But when Christ returns, God's grace will abound in the removal of everything that is evil and the establishment of everything that is good (Rev. 21).

In Christ, we have come under the rule and reign of grace. And that reign is never going to end.

In Christ, We Have a New Destiny

A few years ago, my family was driving down the highway when we passed an enormous cemetery. My oldest daughter was only a couple of years old at the time, and as she stared out the window at the field of tombstones, she asked me, "Daddy, what is that place?"

It doesn't take long in this life before we are confronted with the reality of death. No matter how beautiful and bright this world may sometimes be, we are never far from death's dark shadow. For "just as sin came into the world through one man, and death through sin, . . . so death spread to all men because all sinned" (Rom. 5:12). When Adam opened the door to sin, he opened the door to death.

God warned him, "Of the tree of the knowledge of good and evil you shall not eat, for in the day that you eat of it you shall surely die" (Gen. 2:17). And just as God warned, death followed Adam's rebellion, and death spread throughout all Adam's descendants.

Death comes to us all. It is an inescapable reality we cannot overcome. In Adam, death is our destiny. And if we die under the rule of sin and the condemnation of God, "that place" my daughter asked about is a gateway to an eternal hell of darkness and despair. But in Christ, "that place" is a gateway to an eternal heaven of life and light.

When God saves us, he destines us for an entirely different future. Having been justified by God and placed under the reign of grace, we are now headed toward "eternal life through Jesus Christ our Lord" (Rom. 5:21). Since we are united with Christ, death will not destroy us because it did not destroy him. He passed through death and paved the way for us to everlasting life.

At the end of the Second World War, a British intelligence officer named Payne Best was imprisoned by the Nazis. One of his fellow prisoners was German pastor Dietrich Bonhoeffer. On the Sunday after Easter in 1945, Bonhoeffer led Best and a few others in a short worship service during which he preached about the resurrection of Christ.

And then Best, who survived the war, tells us what happened next. He writes,

> [Bonhoeffer] had hardly finished his last prayer when the door opened and two evil-looking men in civilian clothes came in and said, "Prisoner Bonhoeffer. Get ready to come with us." Those words "come with us"—for all prisoners, they had come to mean one thing only—the scaffold. We bade him good-bye—he drew me aside—"This is the end," he said. "[But] for me the beginning of life."[6]

This is our hope, no matter when our end comes. In Adam, we were destined for eternal death. In Christ, we are destined for eternal life.

6 Eric Metaxas, *Bonhoeffer: Pastor, Martyr, Prophet, Spy* (Thomas Nelson, 2010), 528.

Receive, Rejoice, and Rest

Union with Christ is a doctrine that describes our fundamental position. We were born in Adam, condemned before God, ruled by sin, and destined for death. But in his great mercy, God takes us from our natural position in Adam and transfers us to a new position in Christ. We become members of Christ's family, and this changes everything.

In Christ, we are justified before God, ruled by grace, and destined for life. From now on, when you see those two words, *in Christ,* think of all this. But don't only *think* about it, *believe* it. Union with Christ refers to the *believer's* position in Christ. It's a gift that we receive by faith. And God wants us to understand that this gift is indeed free for all who believe.

The phrase *free gift* shows up five times throughout Romans 5:12–21. Like any good father, God repeats himself to make a point. It's as if he's kneeling before us, laying his hands on our shoulders, looking us in the eye, and asking, "Do you hear what I'm saying? This gift of union with Christ is free. Take it. Receive him."

Apart from Christ, you're still in Adam's family, and your life is still defined by his story. But Christ has come with a new story of redeeming grace. Don't resist. Receive his rescue. And rejoice.

God is after more than our intellect when we explore the doctrine of union with Christ; he is after our affection. Romans 5:12–21 is packed with deep theological truths, and any true engagement with Christian doctrine should not only engage our minds but also enliven our hearts. In Christ, we have received immeasurable grace—grace that will always be greater than our sin (5:20). In Christ, we have been reconciled with God. We are no longer defined by our rebellion; we are righteous in his sight. In Christ, our fear of death has been replaced by the hope of everlasting life. And there is no going back. Our position is permanent. Jesus has taken hold of us, and no one can snatch us out of his hand (John 10:28). This is a doctrine that should make us sing!

So as we receive and rejoice in him, we can stop striving to earn God's favor. We can stop worrying that he will throw up his hands, shout "Enough!" and give up on us. God brought us into Christ, and he will not let us out. We can rest.

At the same time, resting does not mean we may sit back, relax, and remain the same. Union with Christ begins a glorious transformation. In Christ, having died to sin and risen with him, we are able to resist temptation and run after holiness as we never could before. That fight, and that pursuit, is the focus of the next three chapters.

3

Saved to Remember

For the death he died he died to sin, once for all, but the life he lives he lives to God. So you also must consider yourselves dead to sin and alive to God in Christ Jesus.

ROMANS 6:10–11

STEPHEN COVEY, in *The 7 Habits of Highly Effective People*, invites us to imagine the following scene:

> In your mind's eye, see yourself going to the funeral of a loved one. Picture yourself driving to the funeral parlor or chapel, parking the car, and getting out. As you walk inside the building, you notice the flowers,

> the soft organ music. You see the faces of friends and family you pass along the way. You feel the shared sorrow of losing, the joy of having known, that radiates from the hearts of the people there. As you walk down to the front of the room and look inside the casket, you suddenly come face to face with yourself. This is your funeral.[1]

Striking, isn't it? Covey brings us face-to-face with our own mortality to spur us on toward greater effectiveness. He hopes that if we can picture the end of our lives, we will want to make the most of our lives. And I want to do something similar in this chapter.

I want you to see yourself in the casket, but, while Covey urges you to look into the future and consider the fact that you are going to die someday, I want you to look into the past and consider the fact that *you have already died.* Grasping this will spur you on toward greater holiness.

This brings us to the next part of our definition of union with Christ. We have seen that union with Christ refers to the believer's position in Christ established at conversion. Now, in the next few chapters, we see how we

1 Stephen R. Covey, *The 7 Habits of Highly Effective People* (Simon & Schuster, 2020), 110.

experience union with Christ in all of life—especially in the fight against sin.

The Struggle Is Real

Every Christian is struggling with sin. Not some Christians. Not certain delinquent Christians. Every Christian. If you have ever wondered, "Am I the only one?" the answer is no. We are all in this together.

In fact, if you're not fighting sin, you're not following Christ, because Christ calls us to resist the devil (James 4:7), to flee from immorality (1 Cor. 6:18), and to strive for holiness (Heb. 12:14). He commands us to take up the whole armor of God and wage war against sinful practices, habits, and desires (Rom. 8:13; Eph. 6:10–18; Col. 3:5). He tells us to fight.

My guess is that if you picked up this book and have read this far, you are in this fight. You know that the struggle is real. There are times when it feels as though you're making progress and times when it feels as though you're losing ground. There are days you feel as though you are crushing sin and days when you feel as though sin is crushing you. There are some temptations that you find easy to resist and others that rise up and take you down. The struggle never stops. It's like pulling weeds.

Every spring, I renew my commitment to vigilance against the invading army of dandelions, clover, and bull thistle that creep into our lawn and flower beds. Every spring, I tell myself, "This is the year the weeds lose!" But by mid-July, I am ready to give up, spray the occasional Roundup, and wait for winter. The battle is relentless—just like the battle against sin.

So why not give up? After all, Christ came into the world to save sinners (1 Tim. 1:15). Why not just embrace our sinful identity, resign ourselves to the way things are, and bank our hopes on God's promise to forgive? In other words, why not continue in sin so that grace may abound (Rom. 6:1)?

The reason is that, in Christ, God has done more than forgive us (though he certainly has not done less). In Christ, God has empowered us for a whole new way of life. And the more we can comprehend our union with Christ, the more we will come to see that giving up and continuing in sin is illogical, inappropriate, and ultimately impossible.

Comprehension is the key. If you are feeling despondent, defeated, or demotivated in your battle against temptation, thinking about your union with Christ will help you. You might be inclined to say, "Really? There is sin to defeat. There is holiness to pursue. And you're suggesting that the first thing I do about this is *think*?" Yes, that's right.

But I'm not simply suggesting it. The Bible commands it.

The Command to Consider

For the first five and a half chapters of Romans, Paul does not write a single command or issue a single imperative. He leads us into the heights of Christian theology. He shows us the devastating effects of the fall and the incomparable mercy of God. Then, he comes to his first point of application: "Consider yourselves dead to sin and alive to God in Christ Jesus" (Rom. 6:11).

The first command in Paul's letter is the command to *consider*—to reflect, ponder, and think. Paul commands us to *think* about our union with Christ, because the more we do so, the more confidence we will find as we wage war against sin and run hard after holiness.

What exactly is it about our union with Christ that Paul commands us to consider? We ought to continually meditate on the reality that we have died with Christ and have risen with him.

Consider Yourself Dead to Sin

As believers in Christ, we are so closely identified with Christ that it is possible to say we died with him. We have been "united with him in a death like his" (Rom. 6:5). Jesus died, and so have we. What does this mean? We began to explore this truth in chapter 1, but let's press further.

First, it means our old life is over. Our old self was crucified with him (6:6).

Go back two thousand years in your imagination. Picture Golgotha. See the crowd of soldiers and religious leaders and weeping women. See Jesus hanging on the cross. But he is not alone. Your "old self" is hanging there too.

Your "old self" is the person you used to be in Adam, your old life in your old position. It is the person who was ruled and dominated by sin, who stood condemned before God, who was destined for everlasting death (Rom. 5:12–21; 1 Cor. 15:22). But that person is gone. He was crucified with Christ. She was crucified with Christ.

The apostle Paul speaks about this autobiographically when he writes, "I have been crucified with Christ. It is no longer I who live, but Christ who lives in me" (Gal. 2:20). He's saying, "Have you heard of Saul of Tarsus? That notorious persecutor of the church? That insolent opponent of Christ? Well, he is gone now. He was crucified and buried with Jesus." We can say the same thing. Our old self was crucified with Christ. That life is over, which means our bondage to sin is over too.

Imagine that you once had the world's worst boss. He was rude. He was demanding. He was a tyrant. You dreaded going to work. And yet you felt totally trapped in this job with no prospect of change on the horizon. So you stuck it out, day after miserable day—until one day, unexpectedly, you received a job offer from a new company. You jumped at the opportunity, transferring to the new position, and that horrible season of work ended.

There is only one problem—your new company is in the same building as your old company. Not only that, but your new office is also on the same floor as your old one. So you often find yourself bumping into your old boss in the hallway and on the elevator. One day he sees you and starts barking orders at you. He demands that you listen to him. What will you say?

You will naturally say, "No! You are not my boss anymore!"

In Christ, sin is not our boss anymore. We still live in this fallen world where sin is present. We still bump into sin all the time. But we have a new position in Christ. We are now able to say "no" to sin's demands.

It was not always this way. We were once enslaved to sin (John 8:34). We might have thought we were experiencing liberty when we were rebelling against God. We may have boasted in our autonomy as we refused to listen to God. We may have issued our "declaration of independence from

God,"[2] but we were not free. We were held captive by the great tyrant called sin—until we were united with Christ.

Now, because we are united to Christ, "We know that our old self was crucified with him" (Rom. 6:6). Why did this happen? "In order that the body of sin might be brought to nothing, so that we would no longer be enslaved to sin. For one who has died has been set free from sin" (6:6–7).

Before we were united with Christ, our bodies and all our faculties were ruled by sin. But we died. Our old lives under the rule of sin ended. And sin lost its dominating power over us. We have been set free.

Does this mean we will never sin again? No. We are still tempted to sin, we are still capable of sin, and we still commit sins (Ps. 19:13; James 1:14; 1 John 1:8). As Thomas Schreiner says, "What has been shattered is not the *presence* of sin but its *mastery* over believers."[3] Since sin's mastery over us has been brought to nothing, we are capable of resisting sin as we never could before.

Sin is not your boss anymore. So when sin makes its demands, you really can say, "No!" You can resist because your old

2 Michael Horton, *Putting Amazing Back into Grace* (Baker, 2011), 47.

3 Thomas R. Schreiner, *Romans*, 2nd ed., Baker Exegetical Commentary on the New Testament, ed. Joshua Jipp and Robert W. Yarbrough (Baker Academic, 2018), 318. Emphasis added.

self was crucified with Christ. Your former life in bondage to sin has been brought to nothing (Rom. 6:6). And the more we reflect on and rejoice in this truth, the more strength we will find to fight sin. We could call this "the power of negative thinking." You and I must consider ourselves dead to sin in Christ Jesus.

But there is positive thinking for us to do as well.

Consider Yourself Alive to God

Prior to his conversion, Paul was a serious sinner (1 Tim. 1:15–16). He raged against Christ, and he hated Christians. Yet he himself was in bondage to sin. But after he came to believe in Christ, Paul died with Christ. His old life in slavery to sin ended, and a whole new life began. Looking back, Paul could now say, "But by the grace of God I am what I am, and his grace toward me was not in vain" (1 Cor. 15:10).

Everyone who is united with Christ can say the same thing. By the grace of God, we are who we are. We are not who we once used to be. The question is: Who are we? To answer this question, remember that the command in Romans 6:11 involves two parts: Consider yourself "dead to sin and *alive to God in Christ Jesus.*" Just as we have gone through a death like his, we have also entered a new life like his. And "the life [Jesus] lives he lives to God" (Rom. 6:10).

Jesus lives for the glory of God. His every desire is set on doing the will of his Father (John 4:34). And in union with Christ, we are alive to God too. Like Jesus, we also live for the glory of God. Yes, we all fall short (Rom. 3:23), but that is not the whole story. We have been born again (1 Pet. 1:23). We are new creations (2 Cor. 5:17). We walk in newness of life (Rom. 6:4).

When God looks at us, who does he see? People who are dead in sin? No. He sees people who are alive in Christ. He sees people who are set apart for his good purposes in this world (Eph. 2:10; cf. 1 Cor. 10:31). And there is a biblical word for people like this: *saints*.

Are you comfortable calling yourself a saint?

Many of us would say, "Paul was a saint. My grandmother was a saint. But me? Not so much." The reason for our negative response is likely a faulty definition. A lot of people reserve the word *saint* for some special class of super-spiritual Christians. But that's not what the word means. A saint is someone whose life has been set apart and dedicated to God. A saint is someone alive to God in Christ Jesus. A saint is simply a Christian.

We see this all over the New Testament. The word *saint* appears over forty times in Paul's letters, and it always describes believers. Regular believers. Not some unique class of believers. For example, Paul begins his letter to the Romans by addressing "all those in Rome who are loved by God and called to be saints" (Rom. 1:7; cf. 1 Cor. 1:2; 2 Cor. 1:1; Eph. 1:1; Phil. 1:1; Col. 1:2). Every Christian in Rome is loved by God. Every Christian in Rome is a saint in God's sight. And the same is true about every Christian reading this book.

Sinner is not our defining label anymore. We are saints. Saints who sin, but saints nonetheless.

This means that when God calls us to be holy, he is not commanding us to pursue an identity that we may or may not attain. He is calling us to live out the identity we already have. He is not calling us to become something we are not. He is calling us to be who we are in Christ Jesus.

This has always been the motivation for God's people to pursue holy living. Even in the Old Testament, God saved Israel out of bondage and slavery. He made them his own treasured possession. Only after rescuing his people by his grace did he give them the law as a guide (Ex. 20:1–17). This principle applies to New Testament believers as well. Consider that, in Christ, your old life in bondage to sin is over. Consider that, in Christ, your new life dedicated to God has begun. Consider that you are a saint. And then, act accordingly.

A few years ago, I was taking a weeklong class with some fellow pastors. During one of the breaks, one of my classmates named Sam Daniels[4] got a call from his wife. His young son was disobeying and needed a little long-distance fatherly instruction. As Sam and I walked down the hall together, I could only hear his side of the conversation. This is what he said:

Son, Mom told me how you've been acting. Let me ask you something: What is your last name? . . .

That's right. Your last name is Daniels. That's who you are. You're a Daniels man. And Daniels men listen to their mothers. Do you understand? . . .

Good. I love you and I forgive you. Now go and obey your mom.

This is a perfect example of the way God motivates us for the fight against sin. As Christians, when we are sinning, we are acting out of step with our identity in Christ. God could say to us:

I see what you are doing. Let me ask you something. What is your identity? . . .

4 I've changed the name for anonymity.

That's right. You are a saint. That's who you are. And saints are done serving sin. Saints honor me. Do you understand? . . .

Good. I love you and I forgive you. Now go and obey me.

God does not tell us, "You must obey so you can become a saint." God does not warn us, "You must keep obeying so that you can continue being a saint." God says, "You must obey because you *are* a saint."

This is who you are. You are alive to God in Christ. So live like it.

Preach to Yourself

In the next chapter, we take these truths and apply them to our current temptations. But before we step into the fray and fight our sin, let's remember that Paul's first command in the book of Romans is the command to consider (Rom. 6:11). Before we act, we need to think. We need to mull over this truth and proclaim it to ourselves. D. Martyn Lloyd-Jones reminds us that "the main art in the matter of spiritual living is to know how to handle yourself. You have to take yourself in hand, you have to address yourself, preach to yourself."[5]

5 D. Martyn Lloyd-Jones, *Spiritual Depression: Its Causes and Cure* (Eerdmans, 1965), 21.

Why not take a moment to do that right now? Think about your besetting sin, the temptation that always seems to take you down, the struggle that discourages you more than any other. Then tell yourself, "I have been crucified with Christ. My old self is in the casket, and my bondage is broken. Sin is not my boss anymore. There is not a single temptation I cannot resist. There is not a single pattern of sin that owns me." Remind yourself, "I am dead to sin. And I am alive to God. I am a saint. A saint who sins, sure, but a saint nonetheless."

Preach that sermon to yourself every day. And then, by God's grace and in God's strength, live as though it is true.

4

Saved to Fight

Let not sin therefore reign in your mortal body, to make you obey its passions. Do not present your members to sin as instruments for unrighteousness, but present yourselves to God as those who have been brought from death to life, and your members to God as instruments for righteousness. For sin will have no dominion over you, since you are not under law but under grace.

ROMANS 6:12–14

SEVERAL YEARS AGO, MADtv ran a comedy sketch featuring Bob Newhart as a psychologist meeting with a patient for a therapy session.[1] The patient is a woman battling a crippling

1 "Bob Newhart—STOP IT! The Best Two-Word Coaching You'll Ever Get," posted April 20, 2024, by Life Itself, YouTube, 6 min., 4 sec., https://www.youtube.com/.

claustrophobia. It's her first appointment, and she is quite nervous. Newhart kindly invites her to sit down. He tells her that the session will cost only five dollars and that it will take only five minutes. Then he asks, "How does that sound?"

"That sounds great," she says. "Too good to be true, as a matter of fact."

"Well," Newhart replies, "I can almost guarantee you that our session won't even last the full five minutes."

With that, the session begins. The woman shares her struggle, describing how her claustrophobia keeps her from driving through tunnels and even entering buildings. After listening for a moment, Newhart replies, "All right, I'm going to say two words to you right now. I want you to listen to them very, very carefully. Then, I want you to take them out of the office with you and incorporate them into your life. You ready?"

Somewhat apprehensively, the woman says, "Okay."

And then, Newhart leans in, looks her in the eye, and yells at the top of his lungs, "Stop it!"

Taken aback, the woman asks, "I'm sorry?"

"Stop it!" Newhart shouts back. And for the next several minutes of the sketch, this is all he has to say.

The scene is hilarious because it's so obviously absurd. The woman is facing a significant struggle, she feels powerless against her phobia, and she's looking for real, practical help. What good does it do to tell her to simply "stop it"?

Stop Sinning

Sin is our most significant struggle. Whatever else may trouble us and threaten us, nothing else compares to the power and effects of sin. It rules over us from birth, condemns us before God, and destines us for everlasting death. On our own, we are helpless against it (Rom. 7:23–24).

So praise God that we are not on our own. We are united with Christ.

In Christ, we have come under the rule of grace, we are justified in God's sight, and we are destined for everlasting life (Rom. 5:21). And whenever we trip, stumble, and fall into sin (as we often do), we do not fall out of Christ. We are united with him forever (Rom. 8:38–39).

And yet God's grace in Christ is never an excuse to sin. One might wonder, "Since my failures magnify God's mercy, shouldn't I just keep on sinning?" Scripture's answer is clear: "By no means!" (Rom. 6:2). When it comes to sin, God tells us to stop it.

But thankfully, that's not all he says.

Motivations and Means

Unlike Bob Newhart in the MADtv sketch, God has more to say than "Stop it!" His word is full of motivations and means for the fight against sin and the pursuit of a godly life. In his book *The Hole in Our Holiness*, Kevin DeYoung lists forty different biblical motivations for resisting temptation and walking in obedience, such as gratefully responding to God's mercy (Rom. 12:1), soberly remembering God's judgment (Heb. 10:26–27), and earnestly seeking to imitate God's Son (Eph. 5:1–2).[2] And as God exhorts us, he also equips us with the means to obey (2 Pet. 1:3).

Augustine once prayed, "[God], give me the grace to do as you command."[3] That's a wise request. We cannot keep God's commands by our own strength. Sin is too powerful, and we are too weak. But God gives grace—grace that pardons our sins and grace that empowers us to honor him. God pours out his Spirit to renew our hearts, transform our desires, and cause us to walk in his ways (Ezek. 36:26–27). God gives us his word to teach us what is right, correct us when we are wrong, and guide us into every good work (2 Tim. 3:16–17).

2 Kevin DeYoung, *The Hole in Our Holiness: Filling the Gap Between Gospel Passion and the Pursuit of Godliness* (Crossway, 2012), 57–60.

3 Augustine of Hippo, *Confessions*, trans. Garry Wills (Penguin Books, 1961), 233.

God brings us into his church, which he established to build us up and help us grow into mature believers (Eph. 4:12–13). And most significantly, God unites us with Christ.

In Romans 6:12, Paul says, "Let not sin therefore reign in your mortal body." One helpful strategy whenever you come across the word *therefore* in your Bible is to ask: What's the *therefore* there for? What has been leading to this statement? According to Paul's argument throughout Romans 5:12–6:11, which we have covered over the last few chapters, what should increase our resolve to fight sin? Our union with Christ.

In Christ, we who were once enslaved to sin have become servants of the Lord (6:6–7). We have died to sin and come alive to God (6:11). We are enabled to resist temptation as we never could before (6:2). It is not an overstatement to say that the only reason we can fight sin is because we are in Christ. Union with Christ is an essential means of our growth in godliness.

Union with Christ is also an encouraging motivation for growth. Remember, when God calls us to be holy, he is not commanding us to pursue an identity that we may or may not attain. He is calling us to live out the identity we already have. He is not calling us to become something we are not. He is calling us to be who we are in Christ.

"*Therefore,*" Paul says, "let not sin . . . reign." And then he shows us how.

Six Tactics for the Fight Against Sin

In Romans 6:12–13, Paul applies the truth of union with Christ directly to our battle with temptation. He offers a practical strategy for fighting sin that we can break down into six tactics.

I'd encourage you to bring something specific to mind right now. What is a current temptation in your life? What battle with sin are you waging? Knowing the truth about yourself in Christ, how can you fight? How can you seek to stop it?

Don't Go Back to Prison

Again, Paul writes in Romans 6:12, "Let not sin therefore *reign in your mortal body.*" Until Christ returns or we go to be with him, we live in mortal bodies—bodies that are tainted by sin and tempted to sin. But Paul exhorts us against acting as if sin reigns over our bodies any longer.

Sin used to reign over us. We were slaves to sin, its prisoners (Prov. 5:22; Rom. 6:17). Like a cruel guard, sin once held us captive. But Christ came, paid our penalty, and purchased our freedom (Gal. 5:1). He broke sin's shackles that held us fast, opened the prison doors, and called us out to follow him.

As a result, whenever sin shouts at us to come back inside, to put the chains back on, we can say, "No! You don't rule over me anymore. Christ is my Lord now."

When temptation comes, don't think to yourself, "Sin is inevitable. Its pull is too powerful for me. What's the point of fighting?" Instead, tell yourself, "Sin has lost its authority over me. I belong to Christ. Therefore, I will resist. I will not act as if sin reigns."

Don't Give In to Passion

Romans 6:12 continues, "Let not sin therefore reign in your mortal body, *to make you obey its passions*." Why do we sin? If we know something is wrong—if we know the pain it can inflict on others, the shame it can lay on us, and the dishonor it can bring to the Lord—why do it? Why does temptation come to us with so much power?

Here's the truth, if we're honest enough to admit it: We sin because we want to. Sin entices us by awakening our desires and stirring up passions within us. In the moment of temptation, sin looks appealing.

We see this dynamic at play in the world's first sin. Why did Adam and Eve eat the forbidden fruit? Did they fail to trust God? Yes. Did they listen to Satan? Yes. But they also "saw that the tree was *good* for food, and that it was a *delight* to the eyes, and that the tree was to be *desired* to make one wise" (Gen. 3:6). Adam and Eve sinned because they wanted to. They desired the fruit. Temptation stirred up a passion within them. And they gave in.

Even though we are united to Christ, we sometimes give in too. Until we are released from sin's presence, until we arrive in heaven, we will continue to feel the pull of sin's passions. But since we are united with Christ, we can resist these passions with a new fervor. We are no longer slaves to sin who are bound to obey its commands. We are saints in Christ who are blessed to obey all he commands (Ps. 119:1–3).

And the more we walk with Christ and experience that blessing, the more sin will lose its appeal. We can truly say with the psalmist,

> I delight to do your will, O my God;
> your law is within my heart. (Ps. 40:8)

When temptation comes, admit to yourself, "I want to do this! I desire to sin!" Then pray, "Lord, with all the strength that is mine in Christ, help me hold back my feet from every evil way in order to keep your word, for your testimonies are my joy" (cf. Ps. 119:101, 111).

Don't Fight for the Enemy

Paul continues his exhortation, "Do not present your members to sin as *instruments for unrighteousness*" (Rom. 6:13). This verse is about warfare. Our "members" are the various faculties with which we engage this world—our bodies, our minds, and our words. And since we are united with Christ, we must not use any of our members in a way that would dishonor Christ—as instruments for unrighteousness. The word for "instruments" can also be translated "tools" or "weapons."[4] John uses the same word in his Gospel when he describes how Judas came with a band of soldiers to arrest Jesus "with lanterns and torches and *weapons*" (John 18:3). So when you read Romans 6:13, don't picture an orchestra, picture an army equipped for battle.

As followers of Christ, we are in the Lord's army. We cannot use our bodies, our minds, our words, or any of our members as weapons for unrighteousness. That would be like a soldier abandoning his country and offering himself in service to the enemy. This is why R. C. Sproul refers to sin as cosmic treason.[5]

4 Frederick W. Danker, Walter Bauer, William F. Arndt, and F. Wilbur Gingrich, *Greek-English Lexicon of the New Testament and Other Early Christian Literature*, 3rd ed. (University of Chicago Press, 2000), under ὅπλον.

5 R. C. Sproul, *The Holiness of God* (Tyndale, 1985), 115.

In Christ, we have come out from under sin's awful authority. We now see the destructive power of sin's twisted passions. So we cannot allow ourselves to fight *for* sin. Instead, we must fight *against* it.

This is true in the big battles of our lives, but it's equally true in the small skirmishes too. Sometimes, we see the obvious evils of the world around us. We see flagrant acts of wickedness in other people, and our transgressions seem tame in comparison. But taking up arms against the Lord of the universe is no small thing. And this is what we do every time we engage our members as instruments for unrighteousness, whether that unrighteousness is so blatant that everyone can see it or so subtle that we can barely perceive it ourselves.

When temptation comes, call sin out for what it is. Tell yourself, "Sin is cosmic treason, and I am united with Christ, the one who stands firm against all evil." Then pray, "Lord, help me not use my members to fight against my Savior, to whom I am united by faith. Instead, strengthen me to stand with him against evil."

Embrace God's Authority

My family's summers are full of trips to the pool. And since my kids are little, there are lots of pool rules: Don't run. Don't splash strangers. Don't jump into the deep end without your floaties, forcing Mom to rescue you with all her clothes on (yes, it's happened). The pool is a place of prohibitions. And yet in our better moments of parenting, my wife and I remember that the pool should also be fun. So after we rehearse our list of don'ts, we try to give a few dos. Do a big cannonball off the edge of the pool. Do enjoy a freeze pop from the concession stand. Do go down the water slide until your heart is content.

Sometimes we have the mistaken notion that God's commands are only prohibitions, as if all he said to us was "Don't do this. Avoid that." But that's not true. The Bible is full of positive commands in which God says, "Do this. Pursue that." Romans 6:13 begins with a negative command: "Do not present your members to sin as instruments for unrighteousness." But then the verse shifts to the positive: "[Do] *present yourselves to God*." This is a call to submit to God's authority.

That will not sound positive to everyone. Many people today want total autonomy. They want absolute freedom to determine their own identity, their own morality, and their own destiny.

How can submission be something positive and good? As we've seen throughout this book, a life apart from God's authority is not freedom—it's slavery to that tyrant called sin (John 8:34). But Christ releases us from sin's grasp, unites us to himself, and brings us under the authority of the Father. And God's purposes are always for our good (Rom. 8:28). His commands always lead to blessing and life (Ps. 1). Therefore, we can submit to his authority with great joy (Ps. 100:2; James 4:6–7).

We must submit to his authority because we are united with Christ. Jesus lives for the glory of God. His every desire is set on doing the will of his Father (John 4:34). And in union with him, we live for the glory of God too. Therefore, John Calvin writes, "[Paul] now bids us to present ourselves wholly to God, . . . being ready to receive his commands, and prepared to execute his orders . . . so that all the faculties both of our souls and of our bodies may aspire after nothing but his glory."[6]

When temptation comes, resist by gladly embracing God's good authority. Tell him, "Father, your Son lives to do your will. Help me do the same. Your will is perfect. Help me walk in step with your Spirit to the glory of your name" (Rom. 12:2; Gal. 5:16).

Remember Your Story

Romans 6:13 continues further, "Present yourselves to God as those *who have been brought from death to life.*" In other

6 John Calvin, *Commentary on the Epistle of Paul the Apostle to the Romans*, trans. John Owen, Calvin's Commentaries (1844; Faithlife, 2010), 231.

words, never forget where you came from. Remember your story. You were once in Adam, ruled by sin, condemned before God, and destined for everlasting death. But in his mercy, God brought you into a whole new position. Now you are in Christ, ruled by grace, justified before God, and destined for everlasting life (Rom. 5:12–21; 1 Cor. 15:22).

Our new position was established at conversion. We died with Christ, and our old life in bondage to sin ended (Rom. 6:2–3). We rose with Christ, and our new life in service to God began (6:4). God worked a miracle of grace in our lives, bringing us from death to life. The more we savor the sweetness of this transforming grace, the more temptation will lose its power.

Imagine Lazarus. How do you think he spent the first few days after Jesus called him out of the tomb and brought him back to life? My guess is that he was completely consumed with awe and gratitude. Any temptation probably felt weak compared to his genuine desire to serve the one who brought him from death to life. Yet as time went on, even Lazarus would have struggled again. But when he remembered what happened to him and savored the reality of that grace, he would have surely found fresh determination to honor his Savior. Temptation loses its power as we delight in the sweetness of God's grace.

But time goes on, feelings fade, and our struggles resume. Therefore, we need ways of remembering that we have been brought from death to life. We need regular opportunities to catch fresh glimpses of grace. This is why it's vital to gather on the Lord's Day to sing, pray, read, and sit under the preaching of the word of Christ (Acts 2:42; Col. 3:16). This is why we need the nourishment of the Lord's Table (1 Cor. 11:26). This is why we approach the Scriptures as food for our hungry souls (Ps. 119:20; Matt. 4:4).

When temptation comes, resist sin's passions by savoring God's grace. Stop and remember your story. Remember what God has done for you in Christ. Meditate on how he has brought you from death to life.

Serve the King

Romans 6:13 ends by saying, "Present . . . your members *to God* as instruments for righteousness." Present your members *to God*—"to the King of the ages, immortal, invisible, the only God" (1 Tim. 1:17). In Christ, we are God's servants, and there is no higher purpose or greater privilege in life than to glorify him. What could be better?

We get to present our members to God. We get to bring every part of our lives, lay them before him, and ask, "What would you like to do with these?" And he will not dismiss us because of our weaknesses or say, "I can't do anything with that!" No, he takes what we have to offer, and he uses it for his good purposes (Phil. 2:13). Even more than that, his power is made perfect in our weakness (2 Cor. 12:9). He can turn any piece of who we are and make it into an instrument for righteousness—even the members we once used as weapons against him.

God can transform what has been tarnished. He can take a mind that was once full of unbelief and fill it up with faith. He can take a heart that was once trapped in greed, anger, or lust and release it to pursue generosity, peace, and love. He can take hands that were once used for violence and use them to serve the needy. He can take a mouth that was once prone to slander and cause it to pour forth words that build up and give grace (Eph. 4:29).

God has "delivered us from the domain of darkness and transferred us to the kingdom of his beloved Son" (Col. 1:13). We are united with Christ, the "King of kings and Lord of lords" (Rev. 19:16), and we now strive to "walk in a manner worthy of the Lord, fully pleasing to him" (Col. 1:10).

This means the Christian life is not simply about avoiding sin; it is also about pursuing righteousness. On any given day, we should look for opportunities to use our members in ways that will honor God. But when temptation comes, this is how we fight: We don't go back to prison, give in to sinful passions, or fight for the enemy. Instead, we embrace God's authority, remember our story, and serve the King.

Apply these tactics to the temptation you called to mind at the beginning of this chapter, and by God's grace, you will fight well.

God's Promise

This is a daily battle. This is the fight of your life. But in Christ, you can engage this conflict with all the confidence in the world. Why? Because "sin will have no dominion over you, since you are not under law but under grace" (Rom. 6:14).

God promises that sin will no longer dominate us. How can he say that? We know our weaknesses. We know what we're up against. It surely seems as though sin threatens to overtake and overpower us.

But if we have believed in Christ, we have been united with Christ. And in Christ, we live no longer under the condemnation of the law but under the pardon of God's redeeming grace (8:1–3). We live no longer according to the weakness of our flesh but by the power of God's Holy Spirit (8:4). And when Christ returns, he will remove the very presence of sin from our lives forever (1 John 3:2; Rev. 21:4).

If you are in Christ, sin has no dominion over you now, and it never will again. So shall we continue in sin so that grace may abound? By no means. We must stop it. And in Christ, we can. Believe that with all your heart, and then fight with all your might.

5

Saved to Grow

But thanks be to God, that you who were once slaves of sin have become obedient from the heart to the standard of teaching to which you were committed, and, having been set free from sin, have become slaves of righteousness. . . . For just as you once presented your members as slaves to impurity and to lawlessness leading to more lawlessness, so now present your members as slaves to righteousness leading to sanctification.

ROMANS 6:17–19

DON'T THINK ABOUT a pink elephant.

What just happened? You imagined a pink elephant, didn't you? Me too. You've probably encountered this pink elephant paradox before. It's a fun way of experiencing a frustrating reality: The more we try to avoid thinking about something, the more we think about that very thing. The best way to stop thinking about pink elephants is to start thinking about something else entirely.

Fighting sin is similar. It's important to know which sins you are prone to commit and which temptations are most likely to trip you up. It's wise to name them, confess them, and flee from them. But it's not wise to fixate on them. A preoccupation with sin can often become a path toward sin.

This is why accountability groups sometimes backfire. For example, take a group of well-meaning guys who get together with the shared commitment to battle lust. But their conversation centers on all the things they want to avoid—the sites they won't visit, the movies they won't watch, the places they won't go. They spend the better part of an hour talking about everything that tempts them. And do you know how they feel at the end of their time? Tempted.

Or imagine a recovering alcoholic whose only strategy to avoid alcohol is to *avoid* alcohol. When she goes into the grocery store, she won't go near those aisles. When she's watching TV, she won't watch those commercials. When she's at a family wedding, she repeats two words over and over in her head: *Don't drink.* But the more she tries to suppress the desire, the more allure she feels.

In these scenarios, what will help?

The guys' accountability group needs to shift the conversation from the lust they want to fight to the purity they want to foster. The woman in recovery needs to fill her mind with a positive vision of a sober life, not just the fear of falling off the wagon.

If we want to resist temptation well, we cannot exclusively focus on what we're running from. We must also fix our eyes on what we're running toward (Heb. 12:1–2). In order to starve old desires, we must cultivate new ones. The Christian life is not simply about avoiding sin; it's also about pursuing righteousness. And that pursuit is enabled and empowered by our union with Christ.

Pursuing Righteousness

So far in this book, we've mainly focused on the way we experience union with Christ in the fight against sin. In this chapter, we see how this doctrine also helps us in the pursuit of righteousness.

But wait. Are we really supposed to *pursue* righteousness? Isn't it better to say that we *receive* righteousness? After all, if sin has corrupted my life—if all my righteous deeds are like filthy rags (Isa. 64:6)—doesn't this mean I need a righteousness that's not my own? And doesn't the gospel proclaim that God has clothed me in the righteousness of Christ as a sheer gift of his grace (2 Cor. 5:21)?

Yes! We are declared righteous and have peace with God by grace through faith in Christ alone (Rom. 5:1). This verdict is secure and unchangeable for those in Christ. This is the doctrine of *justification*. But in Romans 6:15–19, Paul's primary focus is on the lifelong process of being conformed more and more to the image of Christ. This is the doctrine of *sanctification*. And here's the difference: Justification describes our righteous *standing*, but sanctification describes our righteous *living*. And while justification requires no work or effort on our part, sanctification does.

So Paul can genuinely speak about an obedience that leads to righteousness (Rom. 6:16). When he tells Timothy to flee youthful passions and pursue righteousness (2 Tim. 2:22), he's not talking about an obedience that leads to justification or contributes to his salvation. He's talking about working hard to grow in godliness out of the unshakable foundation of his position in Christ.

And that growth is part of the experience of union with Christ. When God unites us with Christ, he gives us new desires, a new commitment, and a new purpose.

New Desires

I used to hate coffee. I remember going sledding as a kid one snowy winter morning, and my dad was there with his large cup of joe. I thought it smelled nice, and a warm drink sounded good, so I asked him for a sip. It tasted disgusting. Drinking any more would have been self-inflicted misery. But something changed as I grew older. Now every morning when I wake up and that first drop of fresh brew hits my lips, I am full of delight. I love coffee. I have developed a new desire.

The Christian life is full of new desires. Things that once had no appeal to us—even things that previously repulsed us—begin to delight us.

Think about it. Why do you have any desire to go to church, read your Bible, pray, or use your time and talents to advance the kingdom of Christ? Sure, your motives are often mixed, and your motivation seems to wax and wane. But the desire is there nonetheless. How did that desire get there? It got there because you are united with Christ.

In Christ, God gave us new hearts—new hearts that are still marred by sin's presence but no longer mastered by sin's power, new hearts with new desires to love God, to honor him, and to obey him.

This is precisely what God promised he would do when he said, "I will give you a new heart, and a new spirit I will put within you. And I will remove the heart of stone from your flesh and give you a heart of flesh. And I will put my Spirit within you, and cause you to walk in my statutes and be careful to obey my rules" (Ezek. 36:26–27). When God brings us into Christ, he sends the Spirit of Christ to dwell within us (John 14:16–17). The Spirit produces the fruit of righteousness in our lives (Gal. 5:22–23). The Spirit causes us to walk in God's ways (Gal. 5:16). But this does not mean that we are subjected to a sort of begrudging, forced obedience. No, the Christian life is full of joyful, willing obedience as the Spirit stirs up new desires within us. So Paul says, "Thanks be to God, that you who were once slaves of sin have become *obedient from the heart*" (Rom. 6:17).

Some people have the impression that the Christian life is all about suppressing desires. They think that following Jesus essentially amounts to self-inflicted misery in this life with joy deferred until the life to come. But that's not true. Yes, Christians have sinful desires to resist, but we also have holy desires to indulge.

Consider Jesus. At one point in his ministry, he was encouraged by his disciples to eat after a tiresome journey, but he replied, "My food is to do the will of him who sent me" (John 4:34). Why didn't he say, "*My purpose* is to do the will of him who sent me"? or, "*My duty* is to do the will of him who sent me"? Why "my food"? He didn't mean that he had no need to eat. He was truly human, which included having earthly needs such as food and rest (Matt. 4:2; John 4:6). Rather, he used the analogy of food to demonstrate to his disciples that he earnestly desired to obey the Father. Obedience was his purpose but also his passion. It was his duty but also his delight.

Jesus has a healthy appetite for honoring the Father. And since we are united with him, the same hunger exists in us. Yes, our spiritual palates need improving. Sometimes God's instructions look more like cough syrup than honey. But the more we cultivate and give in to the good desires God has put within our hearts, the more we will discover the sweetness of his commands (Ps. 119:103).

Has this not been your experience? Perhaps you once felt led to share the gospel with someone. You were probably nervous, even resistant. But you obeyed. And as you explained the reason for the hope within you, you found your own faith strengthened, and your desire increased to have more evangelistic conversations.

Maybe you felt compelled to give to a particular ministry. You weighed the possibility, considering the other ways you might use that money. But you obeyed. And as you released the funds in a free act of generosity, you discovered once again that it is more blessed to give than to receive.

The more you follow the promptings of your redeemed heart in the pursuit of righteousness, the more you will desire to pursue righteousness. It will become your food, your passion, your delight. Scottish minister Henry Scougal describes the fulfillment we find in indulging this new hunger: "The most solid and substantial delights that human nature is capable of experiencing, are those that originate in the warm satisfaction of well-placed affections."[1] Our greatest joys come from doing the right thing because we want to do the right thing. And in Christ, God has given us new hearts with new desires for what is holy, pure, and right.

But he doesn't give us these new desires to then stand back and hope that we find our way in the pursuit of a righteous life. He is also deeply committed to ensuring that we make progress.

New Commitment

To fulfill one of my general education requirements in college, I had to take an art class. As I scrolled through the

1 Henry Scougal, *The Life of God in the Soul of Man*, Crossway Short Classics (Crossway, 2022), 76.

list of options on the registration page, I came across a class called Metals. That caught my eye. I imagined forging steel with hammers, anvils, and blazing fires. I pictured the sparks flying as I welded some massive structure together. It sounded awesome.

Apparently, I wasn't the only guy who thought so. On the first day of class, our group of almost exclusively men gathered in the room as our professor handed out the syllabus and introduced the course. And we all shared the same surprise when we discovered that the class would have been more accurately called Jewelry Making.

After getting over our initial disappointment, we went to work. Throughout that semester, we learned how to make molds, melt silver, and pour it properly to create rings. We discovered how to form and fashion a small piece of metal into the image we had designed. When all was said and done, we even found that making jewelry could be quite enjoyable.

As God's people, we are being formed and fashioned into a particular image. Having united us with Christ, the Father is now making us more like Christ through the work of the Spirit. And he will not stop until we attain the "measure of the stature of the fullness of Christ" (Eph. 4:13). Like pressing silver into a mold, God is conforming us to the image of his Son.

If you want to know what that image looks like, look at Scripture. All Scripture points to Christ (Luke 24:27). All Scripture bears witness about Christ (John 5:39). And this is why "all Scripture" is "profitable . . . for training in righteousness" (2 Tim. 3:16). We can think of this training in two ways: First, God trains us. Second, we train ourselves.

Romans 6:17 says, "Thanks be to God, that you who were once slaves of sin have become obedient from the heart to the standard of *teaching to which you were committed*." Don't miss that last phrase. Before you and I ever demonstrated any commitment to Scripture's teaching, God committed us to Scripture's teaching. What does that mean?

Examining how other English Bibles translate Romans 6:17 may provide some more insight. The CSB says, "You obeyed from the heart that pattern of teaching *to which you were handed over*." The NIV says, "You have come to obey from your heart the pattern of teaching *that has now claimed your allegiance*." Notice how the believer is passive in this action. God is the one who acts.

Paul is describing the glorious transformation that occurs when God unites us with Christ. God pulls us out of sin's tutelage and hands us over to Scripture's instructions. God shifts our allegiance from sin's demands to Scripture's commands. God commits us to the standard found in his word so that we might be conformed to the image of his Son.

How does God conform us to the image of Christ? We have already seen the analogy of a metal worker crafting silver. Jesus also uses the analogy of a vine and branches. As we abide in the Son, the Father prunes us as a vinedresser prunes a vine (John 15:1–2). This training, this conforming, means that we must endure bending, pressure, and cutting away. It is difficult to withstand. It might be downright painful at times. But we should be encouraged that the Father prunes only branches that are *already bearing* fruit so that they may bear *more fruit* (15:2). When trials and suffering inevitably come, when sin threatens to undo us, we can trust that God is making us more like Christ amid the challenges. We can become even more receptive to his word as we choose to trust him. Then, enabled by his grace, we continue to strive for holiness (Heb. 12:14).

Therefore, we should also consider the ways we train ourselves (1 Tim. 4:7). Unlike pieces of silver, we are not totally passive in the process of transformation, shaped entirely by the work of another. We have an active part to play in the pursuit of Christlike maturity. We have a responsibility to grow (2 Pet. 3:18). As we open God's word, we can prayerfully ask a series of questions I learned from my pastor: Is there a promise to believe? A sin to avoid? A command to obey? A warning to heed? An example to follow?[2] Then, as the Spirit guides us, we should follow where he leads (John 16:13).

Knowing that God has committed us to the standard of teaching found in Scripture, we commit ourselves to read and apply the Scriptures (2 Tim. 3:16–17; cf. Pss. 1:2; 119:15–16). Knowing that God has claimed our allegiance, we demonstrate our loyalty to him by keeping his commandments (John 14:15; cf. Ps. 119:47). Knowing that he has united us with Christ, we work hard to imitate Christ (Eph. 5:1). After all, he is our Master. And serving him is our new purpose.

New Purpose

In Romans 6:18–19, Paul calls us to live like slaves. He tells us that our purpose in this life is to present ourselves as "slaves to righteousness," which leads to sanctification. How can he say this? Isn't everything about slavery inherently evil?

In the ancient world, slavery was often full of injustice and cruelty. Yet it was not exactly like the chattel slavery we are most familiar with today. When we think of slavery, our minds are drawn to people taken captive against their will—manstealing. But in the first century, a person

2 See Kristen Wetherell, "Q&A: How Pastor Colin Smith Unlocks the Bible," Open the Bible, September 22, 2016, https://openthebible.org/.

who fell into financial hardship might present himself to a master as a slave. He would then serve his master and earn wages until he was able to purchase his freedom once again. So slavery in the Roman Empire, while always tragic, was sometimes voluntary.

It is this image of voluntary slavery that Paul evokes in Romans 6:18–19. Paul recognizes that the illustration has its drawbacks, so he offers a caveat, saying, "I am speaking in human terms, because of your natural limitations" (6:19). In other words, he is using an imperfect analogy to help us understand a significant spiritual reality. In Christ, we belong to God. He is our Master. We are his slaves. Therefore, every aspect of our lives must revolve around achieving his goals.

We cannot freely pursue a life of rebellion against him, using the glory of his grace as an excuse to continue in sin (6:15). If we do that—if we willfully give ourselves over to sin—we are acting like slaves to sin (6:16). But we are no longer slaves to sin. In Christ, we have become slaves of righteousness (6:17).

God has committed our lives to the standard of teaching found in his word. We are bound to obey him. He has also transformed our hearts so that we obey him voluntarily. We have come to see the goodness, justice, and blessing of God's ways. Therefore, we are willing slaves, gladly submitting our lives to the King of the ages and proud to say that we belong to him.

Living as God's slave is the highest calling because serving the King of the universe is the greatest privilege. This is why Paul wears the label as a badge of honor, referring to himself as "a slave of Christ Jesus" (Rom. 1:1 NLT).

Living as God's slave is also the greatest freedom because serving God is what we were made for. A fish is only free when it is bound to the water.[3] A bird is only free when it is bound to the air. And we are only truly free when we are bound to God. Walking according to his will is not an oppressive burden—it is a liberating blessing. Living in obedience to God revives our souls, makes us wise, and fills us with joy (Ps. 19:7–8).

So for all the effort you exert in the fight against sin, run just as hard after righteousness. This is the purpose of your life in Christ.

How Do You Want to Grow?

In the last chapter, I encouraged you to bring a particular temptation to mind so that you might fight it. At the end

3 Timothy Keller (@timkellernyc), "A fish absorbs oxygen from water, not air, so it's free only if it is restricted to water. If a fish is 'freed' from the river and put out on the grass its freedom to move and even live is destroyed. Real freedom is finding the right restrictions, the ones you were designed for," Twitter (now X), January 28, 2022, https://x.com/.

of this chapter, I want to invite you to bring an aspect of Christian virtue to mind so that you might pursue it. What is something you see in Christ, in his word, or in a brother or sister you admire that you want to see more of in your own life? How can you grow in that kind of righteousness?

First, rejoice. Your desire to grow is evidence of God's gracious work in your life. It demonstrates that he has given you a new heart with new desires to walk in his ways. Are your affections for his instructions weaker than you wish? Pray. Pray for God to increase your delight in his commands so that you might pursue righteousness with your whole heart (Ps. 119:10). But never forget to rejoice that the desire is there.

Next, consider how Scripture speaks about the way you want to grow. If you want to grow in humility, meditate on passages such as Philippians 2. If you want to grow in generosity, spend some time reading 2 Corinthians 9. If you want to grow in faith, work through one of the Gospels and watch how Jesus strengthens the faith of his disciples. If you want to grow in hope, read the Exodus narrative to see examples of God's steadfast faithfulness to his imperfect people. If you want to grow in prayer, read the Psalms and learn to pray along. Renewing your mind through the regular reading of God's word will ensure that your standard of righteousness is aligned with God's will (Rom. 12:2).

Finally, knowing that in Christ you have escaped from bondage to sin and entered a new life in service to him, make every effort to grow (2 Pet. 1:3–5). And as you do, trust that God is at work in you, training you to "live self-controlled, upright, and godly lives in the present age" (Titus 2:12). And rest your hope in the truth that this work will one day be complete (Phil. 1:6).

God will finish what he has started. He united you with Christ, and he will make you like Christ. So press on with all the strength that he supplies (Phil. 3:12).

6

Saved to Know

But now that you have been set free from sin
and have become slaves of God, the fruit you get
leads to sanctification and its end, eternal life.
For the wages of sin is death, but the free gift of
God is eternal life in Christ Jesus our Lord.

ROMANS 6:22–23

AS I WRITE THIS CHAPTER, another winter is beginning to settle into Chicagoland. There are plenty of things I enjoy about this season—the holidays, playing with my kids in the snow, and reading by the fireside. But my least favorite part is the way we seem to lose the sun. It's up for fewer hours. It's lower in the horizon. And it's often hidden behind a grey sheet of clouds.

In certain seasons of the Christian life and for various reasons, something similar happens with assurance. There are times when our assurance of salvation burns bright like the sun on a long summer day. But there are other times when our assurance of salvation grows dim. It hides behind some doubt or discouragement. Sometimes we struggle to feel any assurance at all.

And yet just as the sun hidden behind the clouds is still shining, a Christian struggling with assurance is still saved. The question becomes: How can Christians gain that sense of security if they don't have it? This leads us to another blessing of the doctrine of union with Christ.

In the introduction of this book, we saw D. Martyn Lloyd-Jones propose that clearly understanding our union with Christ provides a tremendous sense of assurance, comfort, and hope.[1] In this chapter, I want you to see how that is indeed true. I want you to see how meditating on your union with Christ can cause the clouds of doubt and discouragement to dissipate, allowing the bright sun of assurance to shine on your heart. In Christ, we are free from sin, we will surely bear fruit, and we have an unshakable future. When you know that these things are true, you can rest fully assured.

1 D. Martyn Lloyd-Jones, *Romans 6: The New Man* (Banner of Truth, 1972), 30.

Guaranteed Freedom

One of the most common enemies to Christian assurance is our own sinfulness. We look at our Christian lives and we see how far we still have to go. Sometimes what we see looks so bleak that we wonder if we've really made any progress at all. We might even begin to ask, "Am I truly saved?"

The way we live matters—and as we see later on, it does matter for assurance—but any conversation about assurance that begins with *what we do* is destined for difficulty. It is far better to begin with *what Christ has done* and *who we are* in union with him.

At the end of Romans 6, Paul retraces some of the ground he has already covered regarding our union with Christ. Let's walk with him, reinforcing what we've learned and applying it to the question of assurance.

In Romans 6:20, Paul looks back on our lives before Christ. He makes the striking comment that we were once "free in regard to righteousness." Before we came to faith in Christ, we didn't concern ourselves with living according to God's righteous standards. We lived as if we were independent of his reign. But as we now know, living far from God is not a blessing; it is a curse. It is what John Calvin calls a wretched liberty.[2] It is slavery to sin. But Christ came to set us free.

Imagine a dark dungeon deep inside a mighty fortress. The dungeon is full of captives who are locked behind iron bars with no way out. Then one day, the guards toss another prisoner inside. He's been beaten. He's bloody. He appears to be dead. But astonishingly, the man gets up, looks at the captives, and tells them, "Follow me." Then he kicks open the prison doors and leads them to freedom.

This is what Jesus has done for us. He entered the dark dungeon of death and rose again, leading a host of captives into freedom (Eph. 4:8). And if the Son sets you free, you are free indeed (John 8:36).

The challenge is learning to walk in this new freedom. It's not easy. That tyrant of sin still calls to us, beckoning us to return to the dungeon. He tries to make the dungeon look desirable, hiding his sting behind some pleasurable bait. But we know the truth.

We know sin leads only to death. So when temptation comes, we say, "No." We tell sin, "You are not my captor anymore. I belong to Christ." We take the way of escape (1 Cor. 10:13).

2 John Calvin, *Commentary on the Epistle of Paul the Apostle to the Romans,* trans. John Owen, Calvin's Commentaries (1844; repr., Faithlife, 2010), 241.

In Christ, our relationship to sin has completely changed. Sin no longer owns us. There is no temptation that will inevitably overpower us. We can resist. We can fight because though we were once sin's slaves, we have been set free (Rom. 6:22).

This truth should spur us on in the pursuit of holiness, but remembering that freedom from sin is ours in Christ will also strengthen our sense of assurance. We can rest because even if our experience of this newfound liberty is fraught with failures, it is irreversible.

In Christ, nothing will ever alter our righteous standing before God (8:1). And even when we act as if we are still sin's slave, that is simply not our position anymore. For in Christ, we have "becomes slaves of God" (6:22).

God is our Master now. He redeemed us (Gal. 3:13). He bought us (1 Cor. 6:20). He has taken hold of us, and he will not let us go. No one is able to snatch us out of his hand (John 10:29). I once heard a pastor say, "If you could lose your salvation, you would." We are full of weaknesses, but we are secure in the strength of God's might (Eph. 6:10).

This is one of the greatest reasons for our assurance. I love the way the Heidelberg Catechism puts it. The first question reads, "What is your only comfort in life and in death?" The answer is a balm for the anxious heart: "That I am not my own, but belong—body and soul, in life and in death—to my faithful Savior, Jesus Christ. He has fully paid for all my sins with his precious blood, and has delivered me from the tyranny of the devil."[3] In Christ, we are free from sin. We belong to God. We are secure. And in Christ, we will be fruitful.

Guaranteed Fruit

A few summers ago, my family decided to turn a little corner in the back of our yard into a garden. We pulled the weeds, brushed aside the mulch, and turned over the soil. Then we planted, watered, and waited. But nothing happened. Well, nothing good happened. There were no tomatoes, cucumbers, or peppers to harvest. The only things that grew were more of the weeds we had initially pulled.

Our disappointment was compounded when we compared our sad plot of barren soil with the little farm flourishing in our neighbor's backyard. He had an elevated garden box complete with a motion-sensor sprinkler to keep the squirrels off and a scarecrow to keep other critters away. His neat rows of planted seeds produced an endless supply of vegetables and herbs all summer long. Come fall, he even had a couple of stalks of corn to harvest.

3 "The Heidelberg Catechism," in *Creeds, Confessions, and Catechisms*, ed. Chad Van Dixhoorn (Crossway, 2022), 291 (q. 1).

A sense of fruitlessness is another enemy of assurance. We haven't grown as much as we would like. We still give in to angry outbursts, greedy impulses, and impure thoughts. We incessantly worry about the future and can't seem to trust God. When we look at our lives and struggle to see much evidence of God's transforming grace, we may feel discouraged. And when we look at others who seem to produce an abundance of fruit, we may be tempted to despair. Once again, we might ask ourselves, "Am I really saved?"

There's no question: The fruit produced in our lives matters. Jesus made this abundantly clear with two illustrations in Matthew 7:15–20. While he primarily addresses false teachers in this passage, his words can certainly be applied to false believers—those who claim to know him but are actually far from him.

The first illustration is of grapes and figs. Jesus asks, "Are grapes gathered from thornbushes, or figs from thistles?" (7:16). My backyard was once full of buckthorn. Buckthorn is a shrub that can grow to look like a small tree, and it produces little purple berries that you might mistake for grapes. But they're not grapes; they're toxic little fruits that you don't want to eat. Certain thistles can deceive as well, producing flowers that look like figs from a distance. But once you get up close, you realize there's no food there at all.

Jesus says that this is what false believers are like. They might have an appearance of godliness. But their lack of real fruit will eventually give them away.

The second illustration makes the same point. Jesus says, "Every healthy tree bears good fruit, but the diseased tree bears bad fruit" (7:17). Here in the Midwest, lots of us go apple picking in the fall. And if you walk into an orchard and find a tree with beautiful, crisp, red apples, you know the tree is healthy. But if you find another tree where the apples have strange brown spots, and some are even turning black, you know the tree is diseased. It has black rot, and you don't want to eat from it. Similarly, Jesus says of false believers, "You will recognize them by their fruits" (7:20).

So it's important to humbly, honestly assess the fruit of our lives. It's also important, however, that we do not become overly introspective or unduly critical. Overanalyzing how productive we are in our Christian walk, seeking to tally up our sanctification scores for the day, can cause our assurance to waver. When that happens, considering our union with Christ will help.

Before we were united with Christ, we were fruitless. We were like buckthorn and thistle, producing nothing of value. Worse, we were like apple trees with black rot, bringing forth evidence only of a life marred by depravity. So Paul asks about our former lives, "What fruit were you getting at that time from the things of which you are now ashamed? For the end of those things is death" (Rom. 6:21).

Many of us look back on our lives before Christ and feel ashamed. Some look back and see a lifestyle of flagrant rebellion against God. We might even still feel the lingering shame of a long-broken pattern of sin. Others look back and see a life full of self-righteousness. No, we were not practicing *every* possible evil. Our lives may have even looked good by many people's standards. But we were not producing any of the fruit that pleases God. If we remained that way, our lives would have ended in eternal death.

But here is the wonderful promise of union with Christ: "Now that you have been set free from sin and have become slaves of God, the fruit you get leads to sanctification and its end, eternal life" (Rom. 6:22). In Christ, we will bear fruit because we are connected to him like branches grafted into a vine. And he promises, "Whoever abides in me and I in him, he it is that bears much fruit" (John 15:5).

You might say, "Yes, but this is precisely my problem. I don't see much fruit in my life." Fair enough. But I would ask, "Do you see *any*?" If you do, where did it come from?

Let's return to that plot of land my family tried to turn into a garden. I said that nothing grew. But what if I went out there one day and found a little plant shooting up that looked different from the weeds? And what if that little plant eventually produced a single green pepper? Would anyone argue that this plant was a fraud—that it had no evidence of life?

Of course not. Any amount of fruit proves the true nature of the plant. And in the Christian life, even a small amount of authentic fruit demonstrates an authentic faith. If you can see a little love, a jot of joy, a pinch of peace—or any other spiritual fruit growing in your life—take heart. For apart from Christ, you would not produce any of these things (John 15:5).

Sure, others might appear more fruitful than you on the outside. But I believe that Jesus would say to you, "What is that to you? You follow me!" (John 21:22). And as you follow him, the reality of your union with him will manifest itself in a harvest of holiness. Different seasons will produce different yields. But you can rejoice in every bit of fruit you find. For it will lead to your sanctification and its end, eternal life.

Guaranteed Future

The ultimate enemy of Christian assurance is uncertainty about the future. If we don't have confidence that we are headed to heaven when we die, we won't have peace in this life. So how can we be sure that we are safe and secure forever?

Romans 6:23 is the answer. It assures us that "the wages of sin is death, but the free gift of God is eternal life in Christ Jesus our Lord." This verse is like the great crescendo at the end of a piece of music. Paul takes everything we have seen so far in this book and puts it into a single statement. And it's one of the most encouraging, assurance-strengthening statements in the whole Bible.

The verse begins with this sobering reminder: "The wages of sin is death." Sin promises life but brings only death. This was the case in the world's first sin. Adam and Eve rebelled in hopes of gaining a blessing but found only a curse. Ever since that fateful failure, we've been living under sin's destructive power. And we've been adding to Adam's guilt with rebellion of our own, earning condemnation as a result.

Throughout this book, we've talked about sin as a cruel master. Now we see what sin pays its servants. Sin dishes out death to all who deserve it. And we all deserve it. We've all earned it. But there is a way out of it.

"For the wages of sin is death, *but* the free gift of God is eternal life." Mercifully, this verse doesn't say, "the wages of God is eternal life." That would leave us utterly hopeless. We could never earn eternal life. But we don't have to try. Eternal death is a wage we earn, but eternal life is a gift we receive.

I mentioned that I'm writing this chapter at the beginning of winter. This, of course, means that Christmas is coming soon. Our kids are so excited that they've started playing "Christmas morning" as one of their regular games. Two of them pretend to sleep while the third puts gifts under the tree. Then they all "wake up" and rush to open their presents. They can't wait for Christmas Day to come.

When it does, and they open the real presents that my wife and I have for them, we are not going to say, "Well, kids, here's all the stuff you've earned this year." No. A gift, by definition, is freely offered.

And God's gift of eternal life is freely offered to us. We don't earn it. We don't deserve it. But he has wrapped it up and given it to us. And where is God's gift found? It is found "in Christ Jesus our Lord." Therefore, if you are in Christ, you have found eternal life! In fact, you are enjoying eternal life right now. For you have died to sin and have risen with Christ (Rom. 6:11). You know him as your Savior and your Lord who declares, "This is eternal life, that [you know the Father], the only true God, and Jesus Christ whom [he has] sent" (John 17:3).

And this life of knowing Christ and following Christ in union with Christ is never going to end. It's eternal. It's a life you will enjoy forever.

Disperse the Clouds

Union with Christ refers to the believer's position in Christ, established at conversion, experienced in all of life, *and enjoyed forever*. Let this doctrine disperse the clouds of doubt and discouragement from your heart. We can rest assured of our salvation because we are united to our Savior.

He set us free from the tyranny of sin, called us to live in service to him, and will not let us go. He has made us fruitful, pruning what is evil from our lives and producing what is good. He has guaranteed our future, promising to bring us through this life and into the glories of the life to come. We are safe and secure in Christ Jesus our Lord.

7

Saved Together

There is one body and one Spirit—just as you were called to the one hope that belongs to your call—one Lord, one faith, one baptism, one God and Father of all, who is over all and through all and in all.

EPHESIANS 4:4–6

FROM MIDDLE SCHOOL through college, I ran track. In many ways, track is a very personal sport. You run your own race, often in your own lane, hoping to beat your personal record. And yet I would never have stayed with the sport, or advanced in the sport, had it not been for my teammates. In our training, we helped each other in countless ways. We spurred each other on in practices and supported each other through injuries. We celebrated victories together and lamented losses together. We each had our own races to run, but we never ran alone.

Union with Christ is profoundly personal. When God saved you, he united you to his Son. Your old life in bondage to sin ended. Your new life in service to him began. And he has called you—with all the strength he provides—to run with endurance the race that is set before you, striving for holiness (Heb. 12:1, 14). But God has not called you to run alone because when you are united with Christ, you are also united with his people.

We are saved together, and we are sanctified together. As Sinclair Ferguson writes, "The fellowship of the church is the context in which sanctification matures."[1] God has called us to grow in Christlikeness alongside Christ's people. And when we work properly together, we will grow together (Eph. 4:16).

So what will help us work properly together? Let me suggest three answers based on what we've explored in this book. We will help each other in the pursuit of holiness when we remember that in Christ, we are united by story, united in purpose, and united forever.

1 Sinclair B. Ferguson, *Some Pastors and Teachers: Reflecting a Biblical Vision of What Every Minister is Called to Be* (Banner of Truth, 2017), 549.

United by Story

Shared stories have a unique way of binding people together. Ask a husband and wife to tell the story of how they met, and you'll likely see their faces light up. As they recall what happened, each chiming in with personal memories, you might see their eyes meet with fresh expressions of affection or their hands join in a display of unity and love. Remembering their story brings them closer.

Or consider some idyllic small town in America on the Fourth of July. The members of the community, often isolated in the busyness of everyday life, come together for a morning parade. They smile and cheer for their school band and their veterans. Throughout the day, neighbors, friends, and families gather for backyard barbeques. And that night, everyone is together again for the fireworks. What's causing this unusual display of camaraderie? A shared story. July Fourth is not just America's Independence Day, it's *their* Independence Day.

Shared stories foster unity. And in the church, we have a shared story. When we considered our story in the early chapters of this book, we focused on the personal, individual dynamic. That's important because our personal, individual relationship with Jesus is important. As believers, we can each say, "I have been crucified with Christ," and, "I live by faith in the Son of God, who loved me and gave himself for me" (Gal. 2:20). Again, union with Christ is profoundly personal.

And yet union with Christ also brings us into a shared story with all God's people. Romans 6 makes this abundantly clear. In fact, it's so obvious that sometimes we read right past it. Look at the first four verses again and notice the pronouns:

> What shall *we* say then? Are *we* to continue in sin that grace may abound? By no means! How can *we* who died to sin still live in it? Do you not know that *all of us* who have been baptized into Christ Jesus were baptized into his death? *We* were buried therefore with him by baptism into death, in order that, just as Christ was raised from the dead by the glory of the Father, *we* too might walk in newness of life. (Rom. 6:1–4)

Do you see the shared story? We, the church, have died to sin. We, the church, have been baptized into Christ Jesus. We, the church, have been buried with him and have risen with him to walk in newness of life. This is *our* testimony. Remembering this shared story will help us foster unity. And we surely need help in the pursuit of unity.

Unfortunately, as we live in this divided world, we find that our communities of faith are not immune to division either. This is not a new challenge for churches. Writing to the believers in Corinth, Paul says with a heavy heart, "I hear that there are divisions among you" (1 Cor. 11:18). Our relationships within the church get strained—sometimes even severed—by pride, cruelty, impatience, and hostility. But God calls us to a more excellent way. He urges us to "walk in a manner worthy of the calling to which [we] have been called, with all humility and gentleness, with patience, bearing with one another in love, eager to maintain the unity of the Spirit in the bond of peace" (Eph. 4:1–3).

How do we foster humility toward our brothers and sisters? One way is by remembering our shared story. We were all once enslaved to sin. We all experienced the same dramatic rescue. None of us has received any less saving than anyone else, because none of us needed any less saving than anyone else. Therefore, there's no room for pride.

How do we foster gentleness and patience that we might bear with one another in love? One way is by remembering our shared story. We have all been set free from sin, but we are all still struggling with sin. Sin still tempts us, trips us up, and causes us to stumble. None of us are immune. If we think we are without sin, we have deceived ourselves (1 John 1:8).

And when we fall, we don't need fellow believers to kick us when we're down or guilt us into insincere repentance.

We need brothers and sisters who are willing to hang in there with us, to pray for us, and to remind us of the inexhaustible grace that is ours in Christ.

As followers of Christ, we need to remember our shared story. Again, this is why assembling to sing, pray, read, and sit under the preached word of Christ is so essential. This is why coming around the Lord's Table as a gathered body is so vital. This is why meeting in smaller groups to open the Scriptures and pray for one another is so helpful. As we fix our collective eyes on the Savior who unites us, we will maintain the unity of his Spirit and the bond of peace. And we will spur one another on in the pursuit of our shared purpose.

United in Purpose

At the end of J. R. R. Tolkien's *The Lord of the Rings*, Frodo, Sam, Merry, and Pippin at last return to their homeland, the Shire. Though the great war has been won and the dark lord vanquished, they still find a remnant of rebels wreaking havoc among their families and friends. Upon meeting one of these enemies, Frodo tells him, "Your day is over . . . the Dark Tower has fallen, and there is a King in Gondor."[2] Frodo

2 J. R. R. Tolkien, *The Lord of the Rings*, part 3, *The Return of the King* (William Morrow, 2021), bk. 6, chap. 8, Kindle.

knows that the wicked men who have invaded his land have no authority there.

But the residents of the Shire aren't so sure. They've grown accustomed to harassment, and they feel helpless to resist. So Frodo's companion Merry declares, "We have got to do something at once. . . . Raise the Shire! . . . Now! Wake all our people! They hate all this, you can see."[3]

Frodo and his friends proceed to "wake up" the slumbering folk of the Shire, assuring them that a good king is on the throne and that they don't need to listen to the demands of their oppressors. In fact, it's time to fight them off and walk in freedom once again.

In Christ, we are free from sin's tyranny. But our enemy has a way of creeping in and gaining a foothold in our lives. If we're not careful, we can begin to believe the lie that we're helpless to do anything about it. We can resign ourselves to the way things are and cease striving for a holy life.

When that happens, we need someone to wake us up. We need someone who will say, "Wake from sleep. . . . The night is far gone; the day is at hand. So then let us cast off the works of darkness. . . . But put on the Lord Jesus Christ, and make no provision for the flesh" (Rom. 13:11–12, 14).

3 Tolkien, *Lord of the Rings*, bk. 6, chap. 8.

We need people who will remind us to fight sin and pursue holiness. And that is why we need the church.

In the church, we all have the same purpose: We are aiming to grow into the "measure of the stature of the fullness of Christ" (Eph. 4:13). Since we are united with him, we want to live like him. But Jesus never intended for us to do this on our own. "Rather, speaking the truth in love, we are to grow up in every way into him who is the head, into Christ, from whom the whole body, joined and held together by every joint with which it is equipped, when each part is working properly, makes the body grow so that it builds itself up in love" (Eph. 4:15–16).

As believers in Christ, we must speak the truth in love. We must remind each other that sin's reign is over, the King is on the throne, and in union with him, we are dead to sin and alive to God (Rom. 6:11). As we do this, we will build one another up.

Consider three examples of what this can look like in our churches. First, when we see a brother caught in any transgression, we can seek to "restore him in a spirit of gentleness" (Gal. 6:1). When we see a sister wandering from the truth, we can work to bring her back (James 5:19–20). We can say, "Friend, I love you, and I'm concerned for you. The way you're living doesn't line up with who you are. You are in

Christ. You are no longer enslaved to sin. You are a servant of the Lord." We can exhort, "Please, don't willfully walk back into sin's prison. Don't give in to sin's passions. Don't fight for the enemy. Embrace God's good authority, remember the story of grace he has worked in your life, and serve your King once again."

Second, when someone comes full of shame and remorse and confesses sin, we can comfort her with this same comfort we have received: that there is "no condemnation for those who are in Christ Jesus" (Rom. 8:1). When we confess our sins, God is "faithful and just to forgive us," and he will "cleanse us from all unrighteousness" (1 John 1:9). We can reassure her that even when our hearts condemn us, God is greater than our hearts (1 John 3:20). God is our Judge, and since he has pardoned us in Christ, we are justified fully. God is also our Father, and since he has adopted us in Christ, we are eternally loved (Rom. 8:38–39).

Third, as we all strive to make progress in the pursuit of holiness, we can spur one another on (Heb. 10:24). Our kids' school athletic teams are nicknamed the Saints. Recently, we attended a volleyball tournament in the school gym and repeatedly heard people shouting, "Let's go, Saints!" The church is a collection of people who are "sanctified in Christ Jesus, called to be saints" (1 Cor. 1:2). In union with Christ, we have been set apart for God's glory and God's good purposes. Yes, we are saints who sin, but we are saints nonetheless.

So as we run shoulder to shoulder in the pursuit of a holy life, we can look left and right and say, "Let's go, saints!" We can remind each other that we're not just miserable sinners. We are not hopeless. We are new creations. We have put on our Lord Jesus Christ, and with all the strength that he supplies, we can follow him. We can make progress.

We need this encouragement if we want to grow. As D. A. Carson writes, "People do not drift toward holiness. Apart from grace-driven effort, people do not gravitate toward godliness."[4] But if we speak the truth in love, seeking to build one another up, and spurring one another on toward holiness, we will grow. We will press on. And one day, we will reach the finish line together.

United Forever

In his most well-known sermon, *The Weight of Glory*, C. S. Lewis says,

> The dullest and most uninteresting person you talk to may one day be a creature which, if you saw it now, you

4 D. A. Carson, *For the Love of God,* vol. 2 (Crossway, 1999), January 23.

> would be strongly tempted to worship, or else a horror and a corruption such as you now meet, if at all, only in a nightmare. All day long we are, in some degree, helping each other to one or other of these destinations. . . . There are no *ordinary* people. You have never talked to a mere mortal.[5]

We're all headed somewhere. Apart from Christ, we were headed toward the grim reality of everlasting death. But in Christ, we are headed toward the glorious destiny of everlasting life. As we saw in the last chapter, we can rest assured of that future because eternal life is a gift we receive, not a wage we earn (Rom. 6:23). It is grace that has brought us safe so far, and it is grace that will lead us home.

And yet God's grace does not give us a free pass to live complacently. No, God's grace transforms us. Having united us to his Son, God conforms us to the likeness of his Son. And with all the strength that he supplies, God calls us to exert real effort in the pursuit of a holy life, which prepares us for the life to come.

One essential purpose of the church is to train us for heaven. J. C. Ryle writes,

5 C. S. Lewis, "The Weight of Glory," in *The Weight of Glory* (HarperCollins, 2001), 45–46.

> Most men hope to go to heaven when they die, but few, it may be feared, take the trouble to consider whether they would enjoy heaven if they got there. Heaven is essentially a holy place; its inhabitants are all holy; its occupations are all holy. To be really happy in heaven, it is clear and plain that we must be somewhat trained and made ready for heaven while we are on earth.[6]

We in the church are to help each other toward that destination. We should feel a real responsibility to assist one another in making progress and to avoid anything that would put a hindrance in someone else's way.

And one day, when we arrive together, we will rejoice together. We will join with the multitude of God's people and say,

> Hallelujah!
> For the Lord our God
>   the Almighty reigns.
> Let us rejoice and exult
>   and give him the glory,
> for the marriage of the Lamb has come,
>   and his Bride has made herself ready;

6 J. C. Ryle, *Holiness: Its Nature, Hindrances, Difficulties, and Roots* (Evangelical Press, 2021), 42.

it was granted her to clothe herself
with fine linen, bright and pure." (Rev. 19:6–8)

The bride has made herself ready. How? She received a gift. It was "*granted* her to clothe herself with fine linen, bright and pure." From beginning to end, our holiness is a gift of God's grace, enabled and empowered by our union with Christ. But she also "[*clothed*] *herself* with fine linen, bright and pure." She accepted it and put it on.

What is this fine linen? It is "the righteous deeds of the saints" (Rev. 19:8). Our righteous deeds could never pardon us from sin. But our righteous deeds do prepare us for heaven. And when we get there, the transformation will be complete. We will see our Savior face-to-face, and we will be like him (1 John 3:2).

Remember this truth the next time you feel discouraged about your own progress. One day, you will shine like the sun in the kingdom of your Father (Matt. 13:43). Also remember this truth the next time you feel frustrated about someone else's progress. That brother will get there, and that sister will be shining too. So how can you help him and encourage her along the way?

United in Christ

Union with Christ is profoundly personal. And yet union with Christ is not merely personal. Every believer shares the same position, the same story of conversion, the same experience of transforming grace, and the same eternal hope.

Union with Christ unites the church. We are united by story, having all been brought from death to life by the mercy of God. We are united in purpose, having been called to pursue holiness in this life as we prepare for the next. And we are united forever.

We must run this race together. The author of Hebrews reminds us, "Therefore, since we are surrounded by so great a cloud of witnesses, let us also lay aside every weight, and sin which clings so closely, and let us run with endurance the race that is set before us, looking to Jesus, the founder and perfecter of our faith" (Heb. 12:1–2).

Do you have a strong connection to your local church? Are you there on the Lord's Day to nourish your soul with the reality of your union with Christ? Are you receiving the strength and encouragement that God's people provide? Are you offering the same to others? Do you continue this connection and fellowship throughout the rest of the week?

We don't have to do this alone. In fact, we can't. But as we strive side by side, we will make progress. In Christ, we will grow together.

Conclusion

Indeed, I count everything as loss because of the surpassing worth of knowing Christ Jesus my Lord. For his sake I have suffered the loss of all things and count them as rubbish, in order that I may gain Christ and be found in him, not having a righteousness of my own that comes from the law, but that which comes through faith in Christ, the righteousness from God that depends on faith—that I may know him and the power of his resurrection, and may share his sufferings, becoming like him in his death, that by any means possible I may attain the resurrection from the dead.

PHILIPPIANS 3:8–11

UNION WITH CHRIST refers to the believer's position in Christ established at conversion, experienced in all of life, and enjoyed forever. It is the source of every spiritual blessing, the power for the pursuit of holiness, and the bedrock of our assurance of salvation.

I hope this book has helped you grow in your understanding of this doctrine so that you might see the magnitude of God's mercy more clearly, fight sin more confidently, and rest in your salvation more completely.

At the same time, our ultimate aim in studying any Christian doctrine is not merely comprehension. Our goal is communing with a person—the person of Christ. That may sound obvious, but J. C. Ryle warns us that "it is possible to have 'union' with Christ and yet to have little if any 'communion' with Him."[1] How might we make that mistake?

Imagine a husband who is determined to know his wife. He investigates her past, researching her ancestry to get a picture of the family legacy into which she was born. He asks her friends and family all about her, getting a good sense of her likes and dislikes, interests and hobbies, strengths and weaknesses. On the coffee table in their home, he finds her diary and, with her permission, reads through the entries. He gains profound insight into her heart—her joys and sorrows, hopes and fears.

But despite all this effort to get to know his wife, he never really spends any time with her. They never go on a date. They

1 J. C. Ryle, *Holiness: Its Nature, Hindrances, Difficulties, and Roots* (Evangelical Press, 2021), 152.

never sit down and talk aside from passing conversation. They barely even see one another. Can this man really say he knows his wife? Of course not. He may know many things *about* her, but he is missing the chance to truly know *her*. Despite the validity of their union, they have very little communion.

This little parable illustrates something we must be conscious of as believers in Christ: Our goal is never simply to know *about* Christ, but to know *Christ*. Knowing him is a treasure of "surpassing worth" (Phil. 3:8). Therefore, having entered union with him, we want to enjoy communion with him. What does such communion look like? It looks like dying and rising.

Dying with Christ

Communion with Christ means that we "share his sufferings, becoming like him in his death" (Phil. 3:10). In this book, we have seen how we become like Christ in his death from the moment we first believe. When we are united with Christ, we die with Christ (Rom. 6:3). The person that we used to be—enslaved to sin and destined for wrath—is crucified, dead, and buried.

But we have also seen that the great challenge of the Christian life is learning to live in a way that accords with this reality. Sin still tempts us, stirs up ungodly passions within us, and demands to rule over us. And we must fight against it. Even though we have been crucified with Christ, we must also learn to take up our cross daily and follow him (Luke 9:23).

But we don't do this alone. We strive for holiness as we remain in communion with Christ. He counsels us through his word. His ears are open to our prayers. His Spirit empowers us. His people surround us. He is always with us, even to the end of the age (Matt. 28:20).

And when the journey is hard, when we are worn down and weary, we remember that we have a sympathetic Savior. He knows our weaknesses. He walked in our flesh. He has been tempted in every respect that we are, though he never sinned (Heb. 4:15). Therefore, as we draw near to him and pursue communion with him, we will "receive mercy and find grace to help in time of need" (Heb. 4:16).

The Christian life is a life of dying. We die to sin. We die to ourselves. But we die with Christ. And since we die with him, we will rise with him.

Rising with Christ

Communion with Christ requires walking with Christ now so that we will enjoy him forever in eternity. It involves following Jesus with this singular goal in mind: "That by any means possible I may attain the resurrection from the dead" (Phil. 3:11).

In this book, we have seen how we rise with Christ the moment we first believe. When we are united with Christ, we are raised to walk in newness of life (Rom. 6:4). In Christ, we are new creations, born again to bear fruit for the glory of our Savior. And it is only as we abide in him—as we commune with him—that we will produce anything of lasting value and worth. Apart from him we can do nothing (John 15:5).

As we walk with him, our lives will produce a harvest of holiness. We will grow. We will make progress. As we live as true disciples learning to imitate our Master, we will gradually be transformed into the image of God's Son. This transformation is certain because "he who began a good work in [us] will bring it to completion at the day of Jesus Christ" (Phil. 1:6).

We rise spiritually in this life. But on the day of Jesus Christ, we will rise bodily, and we will be pure and blameless, "filled with the fruit of righteousness that comes through Jesus Christ, to the glory and praise of God" (Phil. 1:11).

This is our blessed hope in Christ: Having delivered us from sin and united us with his Son, God will bring us into everlasting resurrection life.

The Greatest Gift

Don't ever rest content with mere head knowledge *about* Christ, even if that knowledge is biblically accurate and theologically deep. The Pharisees in Jesus's day searched the Scriptures. They were thoroughly knowledgeable. But Jesus told them that it didn't matter because they were missing *him* (John 5:39–40). If all we have is theoretical knowledge about our Lord, we will find in the end that we have nothing at all.

But if we press on to know him, becoming like him in his death that we might share in his resurrection (Phil. 3:10–11), we will gain immeasurably more than we could ever imagine.

The greatest gift of union with Christ is Christ himself. Our ultimate purpose as his people is to glorify him and enjoy him forever.[2] So pursue communion with the one with whom you are united.

Open the Scriptures, not only to observe his ways but to listen to his voice. Pray without ceasing, not as some perfunctory religious duty but counting it a privilege to speak to your King and Savior. Worship with his people, aware that he is among you when you gather.

2 "The Westminster Shorter Catechism," in *Creeds, Confessions, and Catechisms*, ed. Chad Van Dixhoorn (Crossway, 2022), 411 (q. 1).

And pursue a life of holiness empowered by your union with him. Believe that in Christ, you have all you need to resist sin and run after righteousness. And rejoice in the hope that one day soon, the race will be complete. God will sanctify us completely (1 Thess. 5:23). For in Christ, along with all the ransomed church of God, we are saved to sin no more.

Recommended Resources

ARE YOU INTERESTED in reading more about the doctrine of union with Christ? Here are several resources you might consider. I have divided this list by popular books, chapters within books, and academic books. This is by no means an exhaustive list, but it does highlight several resources that I have found helpful.

Popular Books

Allberry, Sam. *One with My Lord: The Life-Changing Reality of Being in Christ*. Crossway, 2024.

Lloyd-Jones, D. Martyn. *Romans 5: Assurance*. Banner of Truth, 1971.

Lloyd-Jones, D. Martyn. *Romans 6: The New Man*. Banner of Truth, 1972.

Wilbourne, Rankin. *Union with Christ: The Way to Know and Enjoy God*. David C. Cook, 2016.

Book Chapters

Bridges, Jerry. "I Am in Christ." Chap. 2 in *Who Am I? Identity in Christ.* Cruciform, 2012.

DeYoung, Kevin. "Be Who You Are." Chap. 7 in *The Hole in Our Holiness: Filling the Gap Between Gospel Passion and the Pursuit of Godliness.* Crossway, 2012.

Ferguson, Sinclair B. "Christian Spirituality: The Reformed View of Sanctification." Chap. 27 in *Some Pastors and Teachers: Reflecting a Biblical Vision of What Every Minister Is Called to Be.* Banner of Truth, 2017.

Ortlund, Dane C. "Union." Chap. 3 in *Deeper: Real Change for Real Sinners.* Crossway, 2021.

Academic Books

Campbell, Constantine. *Paul and Union with Christ.* Zondervan, 2012.

Johnson, Marcus Peter. *One with Christ.* Crossway, 2013.

Macaskill, Grant. *Living in Union with Christ.* Baker Academic, 2023.

Tannehill, Robert C. *Dying and Rising with Christ.* Wipf & Stock, 1967.

General Index

Scripture Index